THE NEW KNITTING STITCH LIBRARY

THE NEW KNITTING STITCH LIBRARY

Chilton Book Company
Radnor, Pennsylvania

LESLEY STANFIELD

A QUARTO BOOK

Copyright © 1992 Quarto Publishing plc

ISBN 0-8019-8332-0

This book was designed and produced by
Quarto Publishing plc
6 Blundell Street
London N7 9BH

Senior Editor: Honor Head
Art Editor: Anne Fisher
Design: Jane Parker
Photography: Martin Norris
Charts: Jennie Dooge

Art Director: Moira Clinch
Publishing Director: Janet Slingsby

The author would like to send special thanks to
Hilary Underwood and Helen Fraser who helped to knit the
samples·and Sue Horan who checked them.

Typeset by En to En, Kent
Manufactured in Singapore by Bright Arts
Printed in Hong Kong by Leefung

CONTENTS

INTRODUCTION

When I began to gather material for this book I realized that my hundreds of old knitting patterns were a rich source of lost or neglected stitches and that I had a wonderful excuse to browse through them. When recreated the stitch shown sometimes turned out so badly it was easy to see why it had fallen into disuse! However, for every disappointment several lovely stitches emerged from obscurity to be included in this collection.

My own contributions are mostly adaptations of traditional stitch patterns from many countries, an attempt to prove that hand knitting is an evolutionary and not a static art. They reflect my fascination with the inexhaustible variety of effects that can be produced with a pair of knitting needles and a ball of yarn.

The first section of this book is devoted to the simplest formula of all, the combination of knit and purl to make relief stitches, ranging from the abstract to the pictorial. The second section contains some of the highly embossed effects that cables offer. Cabling is probably the most versatile technique there is, and can be used by itself or with other stitch patterns. The third section includes both bobble and lace stitches which are wonderfully complementary. Scattered or clustered together, bobbles enliven the surface of hand knitting, while lacy stitches have a charm of their own, allowing light to pass through and emphasize their fragility. The final section is a miscellany including many twisted stitches (often called "crossed" stitches), which are a sometimes overlooked method of creating linear textures and cable effects without the use of a third needle.

Charts have been used to explain the stitch patterns because they are more concise and explicit than stitch-by-stitch written instructions, although both are used in the early pages as an aid to readers who are unfamiliar with charted instructions. Learning to work from charts is not difficult if it's taken one step at a time. The book is arranged so that each section runs from easy examples at the beginning to more advanced ones at the end. A knitter with basic skills will quickly gain confidence once the principles of working from charts are understood. The charts are fully explained in a section at the beginning of the book, followed by a list of abbreviations and a glossary of symbols.

Before selecting a stitch and casting on, it's important to remember that knitting is about creating a fabric as well as making decorative patterns. Some hand-knitted fabrics are more stable than others, some are more dense, some are open, some expand, and some contract, so it's essential to consider the use that the knitting will be put to when selecting yarn and stitch. Different yarns have been used throughout this book to suggest the characteristics of various stitches but experiment is really the best way to test the suitability of a stitch for a particular purpose. However, don't be inhibited or imagine that there are rules that can't be broken. Many mistakes turn out to be happy accidents, and many a new stitch pattern is the result of an old one being bungled!

The majority of designs in this book are easy to follow and a large chart may be based on repetition rather than complexity. So don't be afraid to tackle something just because it's large scale or looks complicated. Have a go, and happy knitting!

Lesley Stanfield

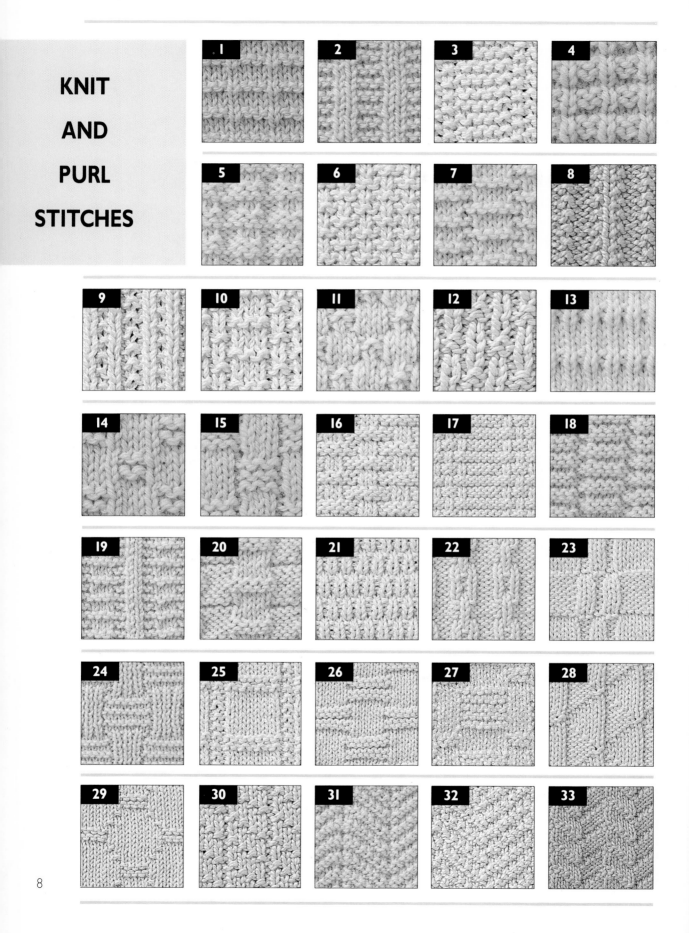

KNIT

AND

PURL

STITCHES

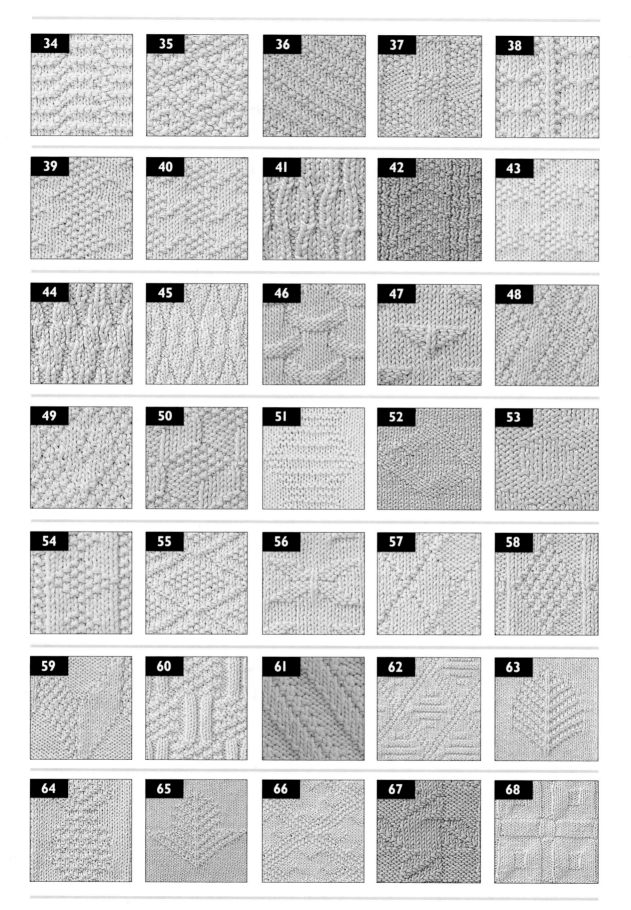

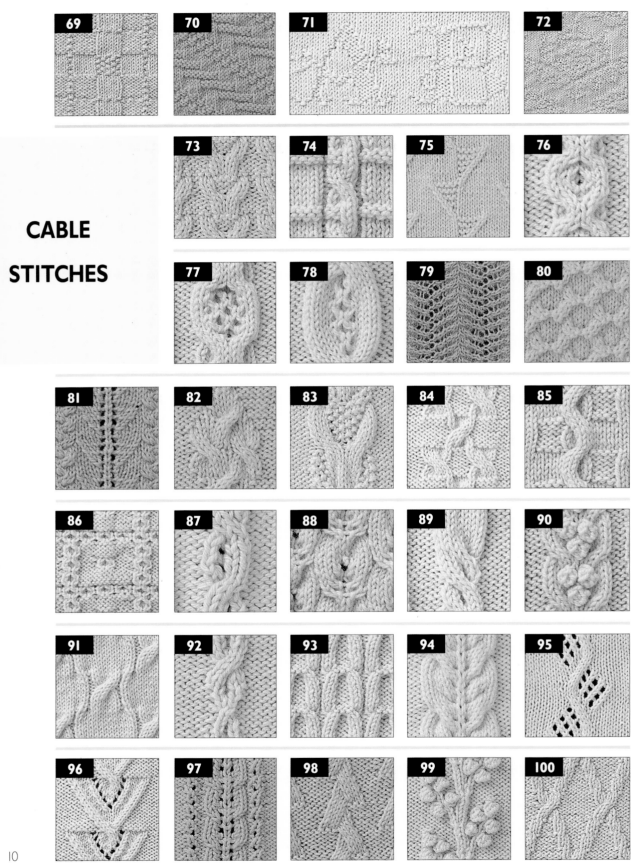

CABLE STITCHES

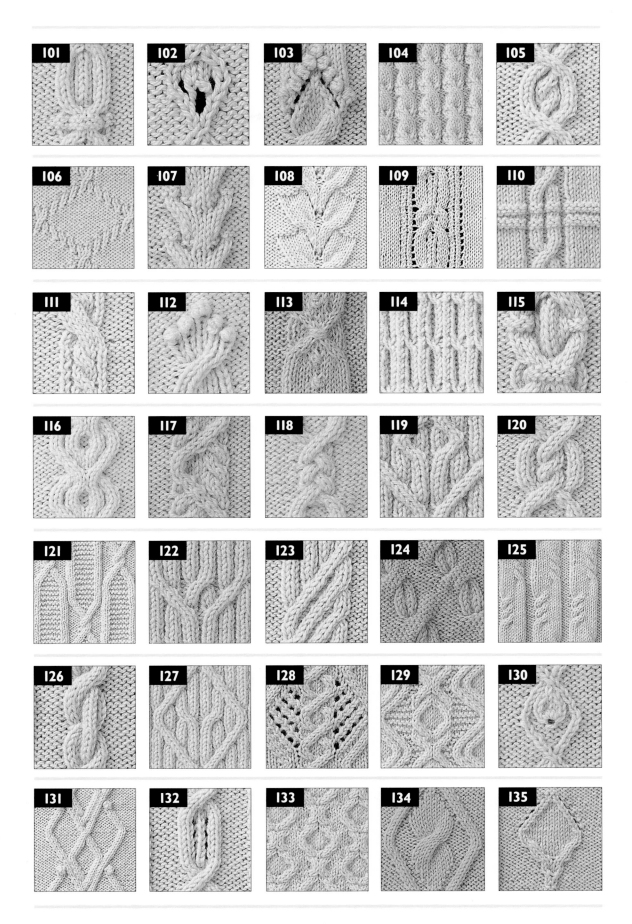

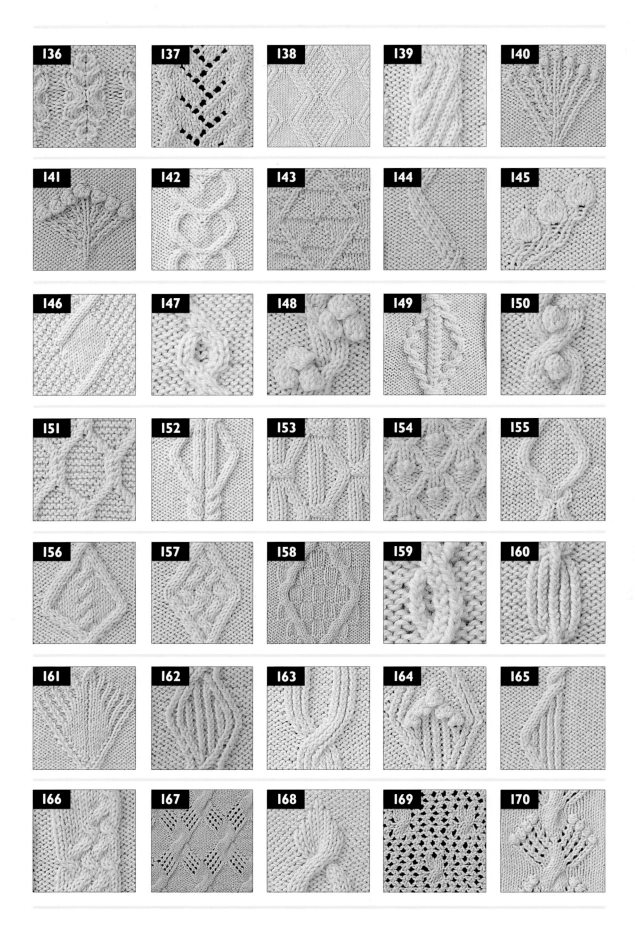

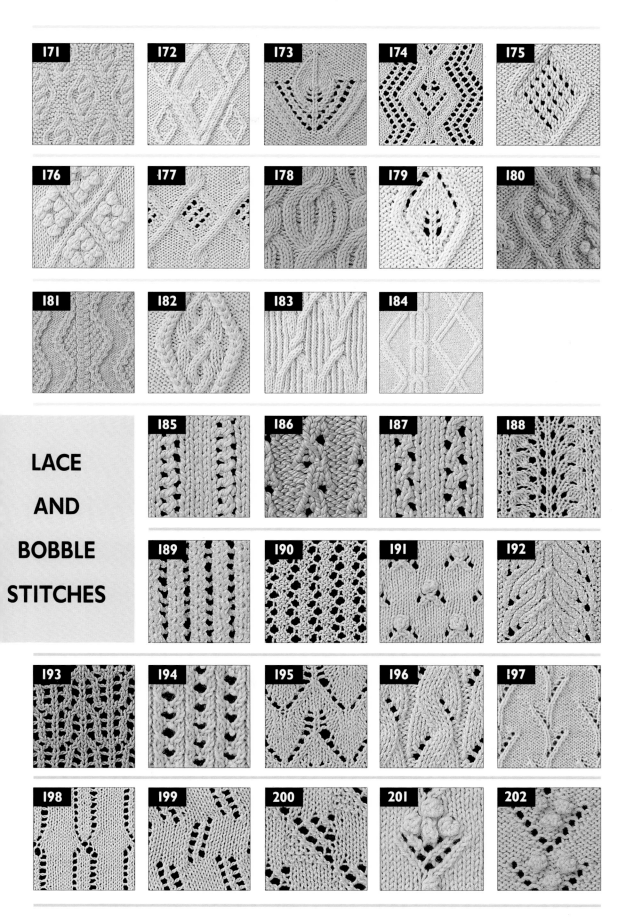

LACE AND BOBBLE STITCHES

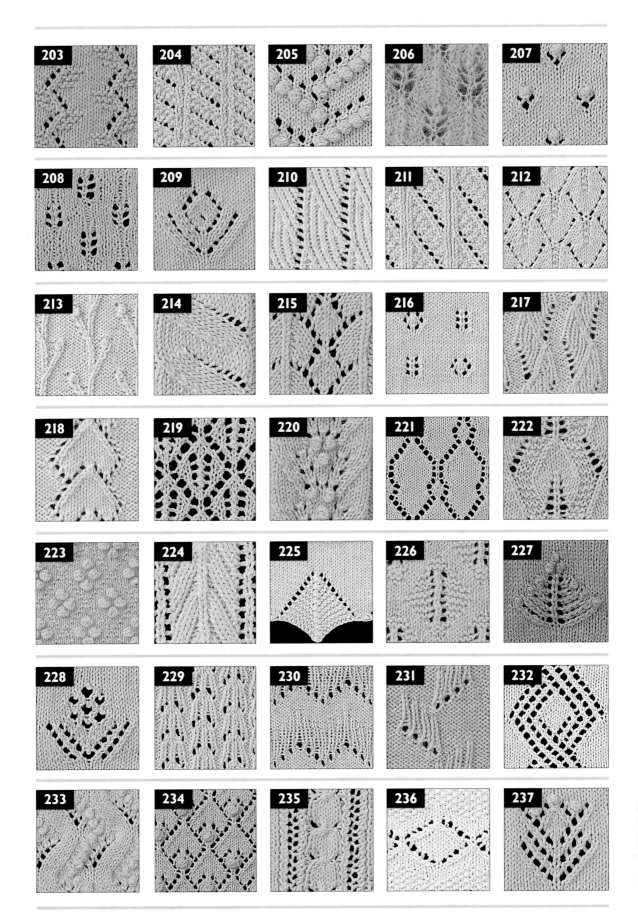

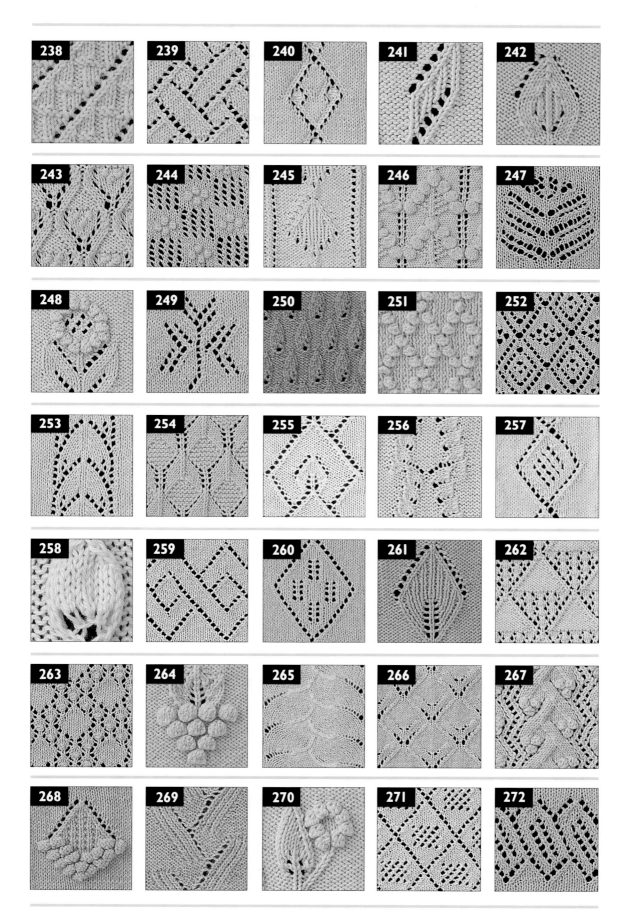

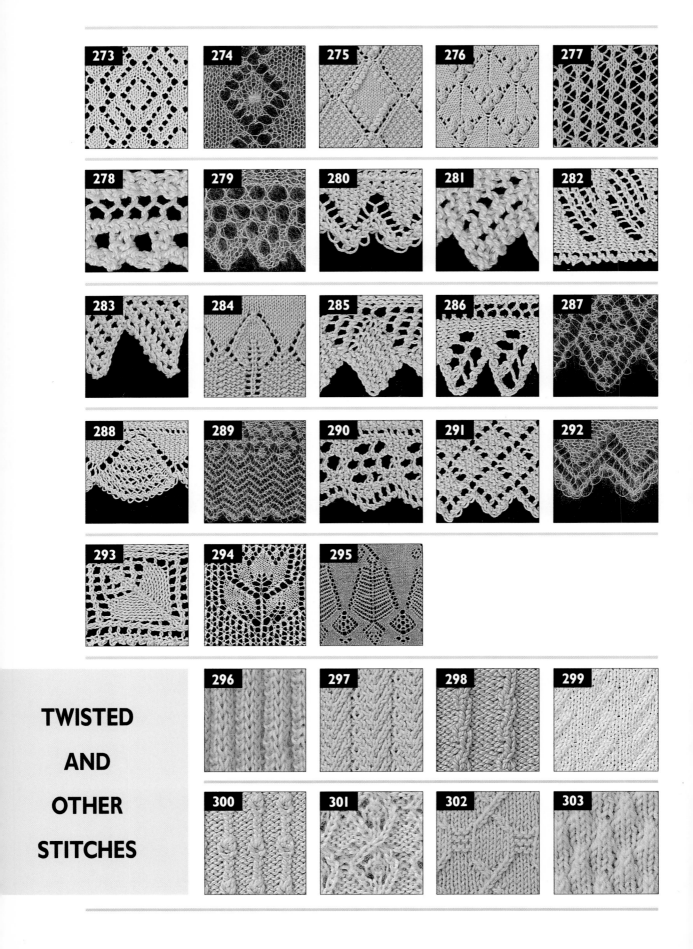

TWISTED

AND

OTHER

STITCHES

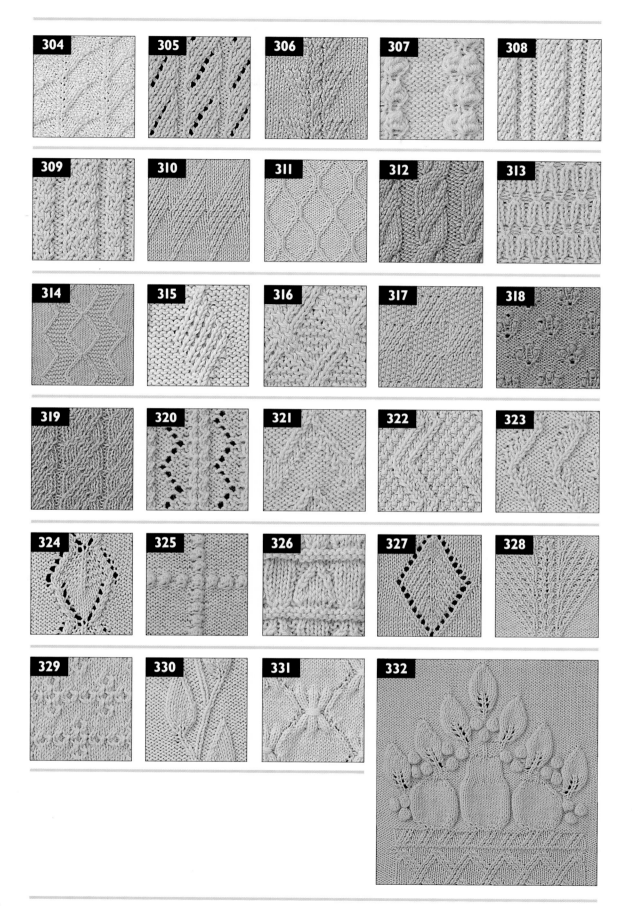

HOW TO USE THE CHARTS

Working from charts has many advantages, the main one being the immediacy with which the relationship between stitches and rows is illustrated. This makes understanding the construction of a stitch pattern and memorizing a repeat much easier. It's also an incentive to adapt existing stitches and invent new ones.

Because the number of different symbols used in any one stitch pattern is small, they can be learned a few at a time as required. All the symbols have been chosen to be pictorial rather than abstract representations of a stitch or technique.

Chart A

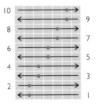

CHART A
• Each square of the chart represents a stitch, and each row of squares represents a row of stitches.
• The numbers up the sides of the chart are row numbers and therefore progress from the bottom to the top like the knitted sample.
• All rows that are numbered on the right-hand side of the chart are read from that side and represent right-side rows.
• All rows that are numbered on the left-hand side of the chart are read from that side and represent wrong-side rows. It's useful to get into the habit of reading all charts in this way, and it's essential when working stitch patterns that are not symmetrical.

Thus, Chart A reads:
1st row (right side): k5, p1, k1. (Worked from right to left.)
2nd row: p1, k1, p5. (Worked from left to right.)
3rd row: k4, p1, k2. (Worked from right to left.)
4th row: p2, k1, p4. . . and so on, reading right-side rows from the right and wrong-side rows from the left.
• If a stitch pattern is to be worked in the round, with right-side facing, all rows are read from the right-hand side.

CHART B
Each symbol within a square indicates the way a stitch is worked. Initially, it may seem confusing that a blank square represents two stitches – knit on a right-side row and purl on a wrong-side row – and that a dot represents two stitches – purl on

Chart Bi

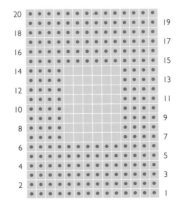

18

Chart Bii

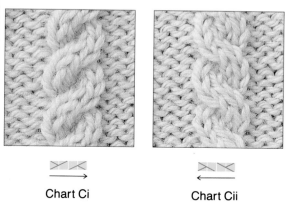

row) have the cable needle held at the front of the work. Thus, in Chart Ci the symbol represents sl (slip) 2 sts onto cable needle and hold at *back*, k2, then k2 from cable needle. In Chart Cii, the symbol represents sl 2 sts onto cable needle and hold at *front*, k2, then k2 from cable needle.

Chart Ci   **Chart Cii**

a right-side row and knit on a wrong-side row. But comparing a knitted sample with its chart reveals the logic of this immediately. The blank squares convey the appearance of the smooth side of the stitch as in stockinette stitch, and the dotted squares convey the appearance of the rounded side of the stitch as in reverse stockinette stitch (see charts and samples Bi and Bii). All that's needed to know whether a stitch is knit or purl is to know which side of the fabric is being worked.

CHART C
Cable symbols extend over the number of stitches involved in the cable cross, so the cable glossary runs from the smallest cables, requiring only two stitches, to those requiring nine stitches. As far as possible, the symbols are drawn to look like the resulting cable. In this collection cables are worked on right-side rows only, and so it helps to remember that diagonals that slope backward (i.e. toward the beginning of the row) have the cable needle held at the back of the work and diagonals that slope forward (i.e. toward the end of the

CHARTS D AND E
To make some charts look more like the resulting cable stitches, additional lines have been drawn in. These are merely to help the eye distinguish between one group of stitches and another and do not affect the working of the stitches. In the same way, lines have been used to distinguish one area from another where symbols are very dense and might be difficult to follow.

Chart D   **Chart E**

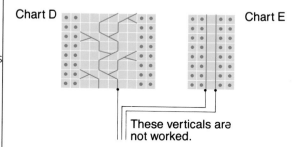

These verticals are not worked.

Any exceptional symbols are explained beside the relevant chart.

CHART F
A blocked-out square represents no stitch at all. For example, a stitch lost by decreasing and not compensated for with an increase. These blocked-out areas are not to be included in any stitch count, and any loss of vertical alignment of stitches in the chart must be ignored.
Thus, F shows a chart that begins with 5 sts, increases 2 sts on both rows 3 and 5, is worked

over 9 sts on rows 6, 7, and 8 before decreasing 2 sts on both rows 9 and 11 to return to 5 sts on row 12.

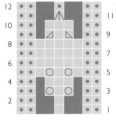

Chart F

CHART G

● An area of a chart that is unshaded and also has a bracket underneath indicates a group of stitches forming a repeat.

● A shaded area indicates stitches that are worked at the beginning or end of a row to balance the repeat.

● The number of stitches required for the repeat is given as a "Multiple of . . . sts" and the number of end stitches as "plus . . . ."

In Chart G, "Multiple of 8 sts plus 1" means cast on a number of stitches divisible by 8 and add 1 more.

Chart G

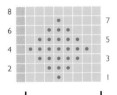

Multiple of 8 sts plus 1.

CHARTS H AND I

An unshaded area underlined by an H-shaped bracket indicates a panel or motif, and shaded areas indicate a notional number of stitches to the sides of the pattern area. In a panel all the rows, of the chart are repeated. A motif may have an odd number of rows, and any number of "background" rows may be worked below and above.

Chart H

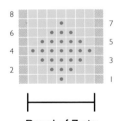

Panel of 7 sts.

Chart I

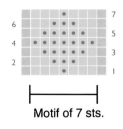

Motif of 7 sts.

GLOSSARY OF SYMBOLS

ABBREVIATIONS

Alt	Alternate. (i.e. every other).
K	Knit.
Psso	Pass slipped st(s) over.
P	Purl.
RS	Right side.
Skpo	Sl 1 st knitwise, k1, pass slipped st over.
Sl	Slip.
St(s)	Stitch(es).
Tbl	Through back of loop(s).
Tog	Together.
T2l	Twist 2 sts to left: taking needle behind work, k in back loop of 2nd st on left-hand needle, k in front of first st; sl both sts off tog.
T2r	Twist 2 sts to right: k2 tog leaving sts on needle, insert right-hand needle between sts just worked and k first st again; sl both sts from needle.
WS	Wrong side.
Yo	Yarn forward and over needle to make a st.

K1 on right-side rows, p1 on wrong-side rows.

P1 on right-side rows, k1 on wrong-side rows.

K1 tbl on right-side rows, p1 tbl on wrong-side rows.

K1 tbl on wrong-side rows.

Sl 1 st purlwise, with yarn behind work.

Sl 1 st purlwise, with yarn in front of work.

Yarn forward and over needle to make a st.

Make a st by picking up strand in front of next st and k it in back.

Make a st by picking up strand in front of next st and p it in back.

Increase 1 st by working k in front, then back, of st.

Increase 1 st by working p in back, then front, of st.

Increase 2 sts by working (k1, p1, k1) in st.

Increase 2 sts by working (k1 tbl, k1) in st, then insert left-hand needle behind the vertical strand running downward between the 2 sts just worked and work this strand k1 tbl.

Multiple increase – method given beside chart.

K2 tog on right-side rows, p2 tog on wrong-side rows.

Skpo on right-side rows, p2 tog tbl on wrong-side rows.

P2 tog on right-side rows, k2 tog on wrong-side rows.

P2 tog tbl on right-side rows.

K3 tog.

K3 tog tbl.

P3 tog.

Sl 1 knitwise, k2 tog, psso.

Sl 2 sts as if to work k2 tog; k1, psso.

Bind off 1 st.

St left on right-hand needle after binding off.

Knot: (k1, p1, k1, p1, k1) in st to make 5 sts from 1, then pass 2nd, 3rd, 4th, and 5th sts, one at a time, over first st.

Large knot: (K1, p1, k1, p1, k1, p1, k1) in st to make 7 sts from 1, pass 2nd, 3rd, 4th, 5th, 6th, and 7th sts, one at a time, over first st.

Small bobble: (k1, p1, k1, p1, k1) in st to make 5 sts from 1, turn, p5, turn; pass 2nd, 3rd, 4th and 5th sts, one at a time, over first st then k in back of this st.

Large bobble: (k1, p1, k1, p1, k1) in st to make 5 sts from 1, turn, p5, turn, k5, turn, p5, turn; pass 2nd, 3rd, 4th and 5th sts over first st then k in back of this st.

Purl bobble: (p in front, back, front, back, front) of st to make 5 sts from 1, turn, k5, turn, p5, turn, k5, turn; pass 2nd, 3rd, 4th, and 5th sts, one at a time, over first st then k in back of this st.

Wide bobble: [k2, turn, p2, turn] twice, [k next st tog with corresponding st of first row of bobble] twice.

Sl 3 sts onto cable needle, wind yarn counterclockwise around base of sts 8 times, ending with yarn at back of work, sl sts onto right-hand needle.

Sl 4 sts onto cable needle, wind yarn counterclockwise around base of sts 4 times, ending with yarn at back of work, sl sts onto right-hand needle.

Sl 5 sts onto cable needle, wind yarn counterclockwise around base of sts 4 times, ending with yarn at back of work, sl sts onto right-hand needle.

Sl 6 sts onto cable needle, wind yarn counterclockwise around base of sts 4 times, ending with yarn at back of work, sl sts onto right-hand needle.

Sl 10 sts onto cable needle, wind yarn counterclockwise around base of sts 4 times, ending with yarn at back of work, sl sts onto right-hand needle.

No stitch.

Twist 2 sts to right: k2 tog, leaving sts on needle, insert right-hand needle between sts

just worked and k first st again; sl both sts off tog.

Twist 2 sts to left: taking needle behind work, k in back loop of 2nd st on left-hand needle, k in front of first st; sl both sts off tog.

Purl twist to right: taking needle to front of work, k 2nd st on left-hand needle, p first st; sl both sts off tog.

Purl twist to left: taking needle behind work, p in back of 2nd st on left-hand needle, k in front of first st; sl both sts off tog.

Twist 3 sts: taking needle to front of work, k 3rd st on left-hand needle, then 2nd st, then first st; sl all sts off tog.

CABLES

Sl 1 st onto cable needle and hold at back, k1, then k1 from cable needle.

Sl 1 st onto cable needle and hold at front, k1, then k1 from cable needle.

Sl 1 st onto cable needle and hold at back, k1, then p1 from cable needle.

Sl 1 st onto cable needle and hold at front, p1, then k1 from cable needle.

Sl 2 sts onto cable needle and hold at back, k1, then k2 from cable needle.

Sl 1 st onto cable needle and hold at front, k2, then k1 from cable needle.

Sl 2 sts onto cable needle and hold at back, k1, then p2 sts from cable needle.

Sl 1 st onto cable needle and hold at front, p2, then k1 st from cable needle.

Sl 2 sts onto cable needle and hold at back, k1, sl last st from cable needle back onto left-hand needle and p this st, then k1 from cable needle.

Sl 1 st onto cable needle and hold at front, k1, p1, then k1 from cable needle.

Sl 1 st onto cable needle and hold at back, k2, then k1 from cable needle.

Sl 2 sts onto cable needle and hold at front, k1, then k2 from cable needle.

Sl 1 st onto cable needle and hold at back, k2, then p1 from cable needle.

Sl 2 sts onto cable needle and hold at front, p1, then k2 from cable needle.

Sl 1 st onto cable needle and hold at back, t2r, then p1 from cable needle.

Sl 2 sts onto cable needle and hold at front, p1, then t2r from cable needle.

Sl 2 sts onto cable needle and hold at back, k2, then k2 from cable needle.

Sl 2 sts onto cable needle and hold at front, k2, then k2 from cable needle.

Sl 2 sts onto cable needle and hold at back, k2, then p2 from cable needle.

Sl 2 sts onto cable needle and hold at front, p2, then k2 from cable needle.

Sl 1 st onto cable needle and hold at back, k3, then p1 from cable needle.

Sl 3 sts onto cable needle and hold at front, p1, then k3 from cable needle.

Sl 3 sts onto cable needle and hold at back, k2, sl last st from cable needle back onto left-hand needle and k this st, then k2 from cable needle.

Sl 2 sts onto first cable needle and hold at front, sl 1 st onto 2nd cable needle and hold at back, k2; k1 from 2nd cable needle then k2 from first cable needle.

Sl 3 sts onto cable needle and hold at back, k2, sl last st from cable needle back onto left-hand needle and p this st, then k2 from cable needle.

Sl 2 sts onto first cable needle and hold at front, sl 1 st onto 2nd cable needle and hold at

back, k2; p1 from 2nd cable needle then k2 from first cable needle.

Sl 1 st onto first cable needle and hold at front, sl 3 sts onto 2nd cable needle and hold at back, k1; p3 from 2nd cable needle, then k1 from first cable needle.

Sl 2 sts onto cable needle and hold at back, k3, then p2 from cable needle.

Sl 3 sts onto cable needle and hold at front, p2, then k3 from cable needle.

Sl 1 st onto cable needle and hold at back, t2r, t2l, then k1 from cable needle.

Sl 4 sts onto cable needle and hold at front, k1, then t2r, t2l from cable needle.

Sl 1 st onto cable needle and hold at back, t2r, t2l, then p1 from cable needle.

Sl 4 sts onto cable needle and hold at front, p1, then t2r, t2l from cable needle.

Sl 1 st onto cable needle and hold at back, t2l, t2r, then p1 from cable needle.

Sl 4 sts onto cable needle and hold at front, p1, then t2l, t2r from cable needle.

Sl 3 sts onto cable needle and hold at back, k3, then k3 from cable needle.

Sl 3 sts onto cable needle and hold at front, k3, then k3 from cable needle.

Sl 4 sts onto cable needle and hold at back, k2, sl last 2 sts from cable needle back onto left-hand needle and p these 2 sts, then k2 from cable needle.

Sl 2 sts onto first cable needle and hold at front, sl 2 sts onto 2nd cable needle and hold at back, k2; p2 from 2nd cable needle then k2 from first cable needle.

Sl 4 sts onto cable needle and hold at back, k3, sl last st from cable needle back onto left-hand needle and k this st, then k3 from cable needle.

Sl 4 sts onto cable needle and hold at back, k3, sl last st from cable needle back onto left-hand needle and p this st, then k3 from cable needle.

Sl 4 sts onto cable needle and hold at back, k4, then k4 from cable needle.

Sl 4 sts onto cable needle and hold at front, k4, then k4 from cable needle.

Sl 5 sts onto cable needle and hold at back, k4 then k5 from cable needle.

Sl 4 sts onto cable needle and hold at back, k5, then k4 from cable needle.

KNIT AND PURL STITCHES

Knit and purl stitches are the basis of all knitting. On their own they offer a tremendous number of possibilities. The smoothness of the "knit" side of the stitch and the roundness of the "purl" side can be contrasted to make textures as varied as seed stitch and brocade. The stitches can be aligned vertically to make ribs or horizontally to make ridges. In turn, these can be combined to make brick patterns and basket weaves.

The very simplest knit and purl textures are sometimes overlooked, but a sweater banded with many small-repeat, grainy stitches would be very attractive. Traditional English fishermen's Guernseys decorated with knit and purl geometrics are enduring classics. Whatever the design, it's advisable to use a smooth, firm yarn and a close gauge to emphasize the contrast between smooth and raised stitches.

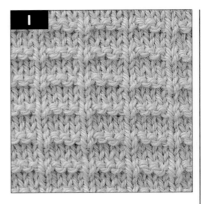

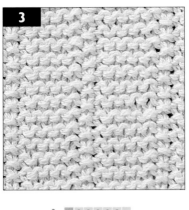

Multiple of 4 sts plus 1.

1st row (right side): k.
2nd row: p.
3rd row: * k1, p3; repeat from * to last st, k1.
4th row: p.
Repeat rows 1–4.

Multiple of 5 sts plus 2.

1st row (right side): * k2, p3; repeat from * to last 2 sts, k2.
2nd row: p.
Repeat rows 1 and 2.

Multiple of 6 sts plus 1.
This stitch is reversible.

1st row (right side): * p1, k5; repeat from * to last st, p1.
2nd row: p1, * k5, p1; repeat from * to end.
Repeat rows 1 and 2.

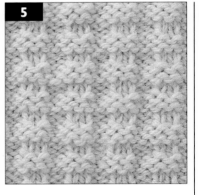

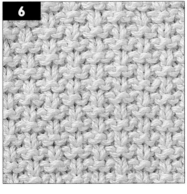

Multiple of 3 sts plus 1.

1st row (right side): * k1, p2; repeat from * to last st, k1.
2nd row: p1, * k2, p1; repeat from * to end.
3rd row: k.
4th row: p.
Repeat rows 1–4.

Multiple of 4 sts plus 2.

1st row (right side): p.
2nd row: k.
3rd row: * k2, p2; repeat from * to last 2 sts, k2.
4th row: p2, * k2, p2; repeat from * to end.
Repeat rows 1–4.

Multiple of 4 sts plus 1.

1st row (right side): * k1, p3; repeat from * to last st, k1.
2nd row: p.
3rd row: * p2, k1, p1; repeat from * to last st, p1.
4th row: p.
Repeat rows 1–4.

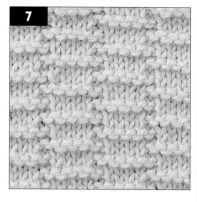

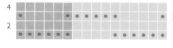

Multiple of 10 sts plus 6.

1st row (right side): * p6, k4; repeat from * to last 6 sts, p6.
2nd row: p.
3rd row: * p1, k4, p5; repeat from * to last 6 sts, p1, k4, p1.
4th row: p.
Repeat rows 1–4.

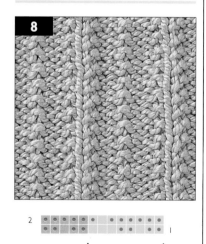

Multiple of 8 sts plus 5.

1st row (right side): * p2, k1, p2, k3; repeat from * to last 5 sts, p2, k1, p2.
2nd row: k5, * k1, p1, k6; repeat from * to end.
Repeat rows 1 and 2.

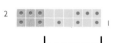

Multiple of 6 sts plus 3.
This stitch is reversible.

1st row (right side): * p1, k1; repeat from * to last st, p1.
2nd row: k3, * p3, k3; repeat from * to end.
Repeat rows 1 and 2.

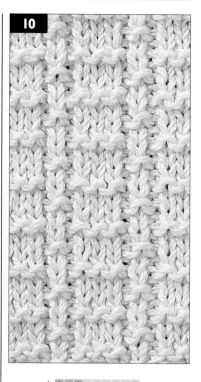

Multiple of 6 sts plus 3.

1st row (right side): * p1, k1, p4; repeat from * to last 3 sts, p1, k1, p1.
2nd row: k1, p1, k1, * p3, k1, p1, k1; repeat from * to end.
3rd row: * p3, k3; repeat from * to last 3 sts, p3.
4th row: k1, p1, k1, * p3, k1, p1, k1; repeat from * to end.
Repeat rows 1–4.

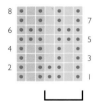

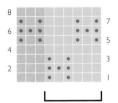

11

Multiple of 6 sts plus 3.

1st and 3rd rows (right side): *
k3, p1, k1, p1; repeat from * to
last 3 sts, k3.
2nd row: p3, * k3, p3; repeat
from * to end.
4th row: p.
5th and 7th rows: * p1, k1, p1,
k3; repeat from * to last 3 sts,
p1, k1, p1.
6th row: k3, * p3, k3; repeat
from * to end.
8th row: p.
Repeat rows 1–8.

12

Multiple of 4 sts plus 3.

1st row (right side): * p1, k1,
p2; repeat from * to last 3 sts,
p1, k1, p1.
2nd row: k1, p1, k1, * k2, p1, k1;
repeat from * to end.
3rd row: * p1, k1; repeat from
* to last st, p1.
4th row: k1, * p1, k1; repeat
from * to end.
5th row: * p3, k1; repeat from
* to last 3 sts, p3.
6th row: k3, * p1, k3; repeat
from * to end.
7th row: as 3rd row.
8th row: as 4th row.
Repeat rows 1–8.

13

Multiple of 2 sts plus 1.

1st and 3rd rows (right side):
k.
2nd and 4th rows: p.
5th row: * k1, p1; repeat from
* to last st, k1.
6th row: p1, * k1, p1; repeat
from * to end.
Repeat rows 1–6.

14

15

16

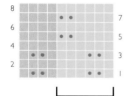

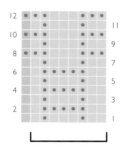

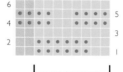

Multiple of 6 sts plus 4.

1st and 3rd rows (right side): *
k1, p2, k3; repeat from * to last
4 sts, k1, p2, k1.
2nd and alt rows: p.
5th and 7th rows: * k4, p2;
repeat from * to last 4 sts, k4.
8th row: p.
Repeat rows 1–8.

Multiple of 8 sts plus 1.

1st, 3rd, 5th, and 7th rows
(right side): * k2, p1, k3, p1, k1;
repeat from * to last st, k1.
2nd, 4th, and 6th rows: p1,
* p1, k5, p2; repeat from * to
end.
8th and 10th rows: k1, * k2,
p3, k3; repeat from * to end.
9th and 11th rows: * k2, p1,
k3, p1, k1; repeat from * to last
st, k1.
12th row: as 8th row.
Repeat rows 1–12.

Multiple of 8 sts plus 2.

1st row (right side): * k2, p6;
repeat from * to last 2 sts, k2.
2nd row: p2, * k6, p2; repeat
from * to end.
3rd row: k.
4th row: k2, * k2, p2, k4;
repeat from * to end.
5th row: * p4, k2, p2; repeat
from * to last 2 sts, p2.
6th row: p.
Repeat rows 1–6.

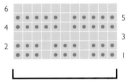

Multiple of 11 sts.

1st row (right side): * p3, [k1, p3] twice; repeat from * to end.
2nd row: * k3, [p1, k3] twice; repeat from * to end.
3rd row: k.
4th row: * k5, p1, k5; repeat from * to end.
5th row: * p5, k1, p5; repeat from * to end.
6th row: p.
Repeat rows 1–6.

Multiple of 12 sts plus 8.

1st row (right side): * p8, k4; repeat from * to last 8 sts, p8.
2nd row: k8, * p4, k8; repeat from * to end.
3rd row: * p2, k4, p6; repeat from * to last 8 sts, p2, k4, p2.
4th row: k2, p4, k2, * k6, p4, k2; repeat from * to end.
Repeat rows 1–4.

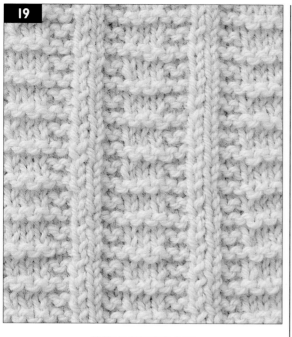

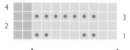

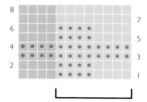

Multiple of 9 sts plus 2.

1st row (right side): * k2, p2, k3, p2; repeat from * to last 2 sts, k2.
2nd row: p.
3rd row: * k2, p7; repeat from * to last 2 sts, k2.
4th row: p.
Repeat rows 1–4.

Multiple of 8 sts plus 4. This stitch is reversible.

1st row (right side): * k4, p4; repeat from * to last 4 sts, k4.
2nd and alt rows: k all k sts and p all p sts as they appear.
3rd row: p.
5th row: as first row.
7th row: k.
8th row: as 2nd row.
Repeat rows 1–8.

21

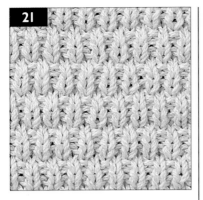

Multiple of 2 sts plus 1.

22

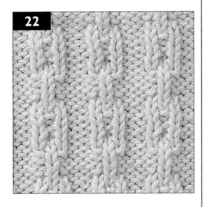

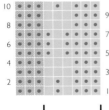

Multiple of 6 sts plus 3.

23

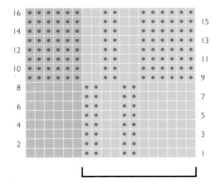

Multiple of 12 sts plus 6.

24

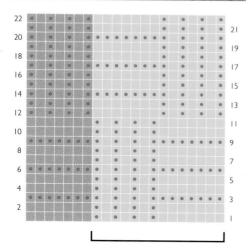

Multiple of 14 sts plus 7.

25

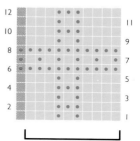

Multiple of 10 sts plus 1.

26

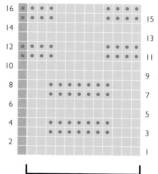

Multiple of 12 sts plus 1.

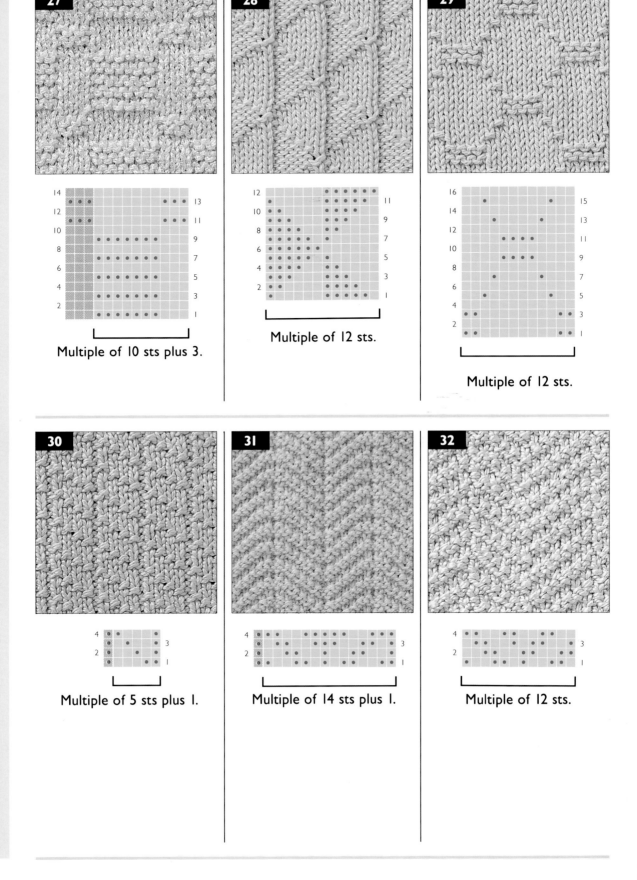

27

Multiple of 10 sts plus 3.

28

Multiple of 12 sts.

29

Multiple of 12 sts.

30

Multiple of 5 sts plus 1.

31

Multiple of 14 sts plus 1.

32

Multiple of 12 sts.

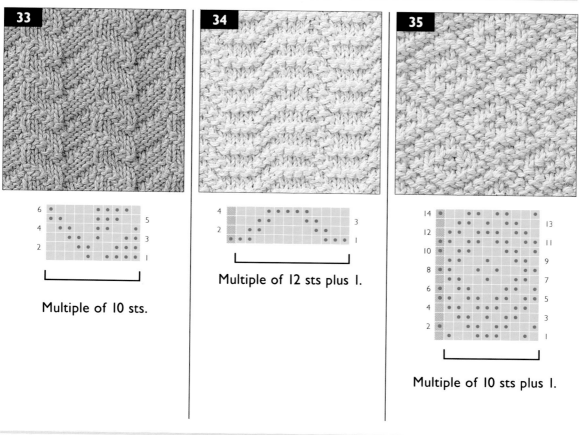

33

Multiple of 10 sts.

34

Multiple of 12 sts plus 1.

35

Multiple of 10 sts plus 1.

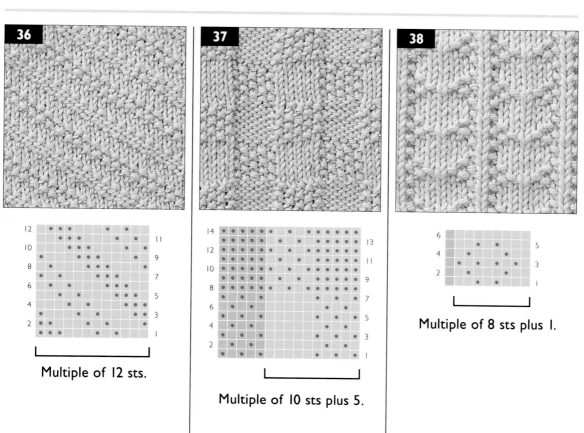

36

Multiple of 12 sts.

37

Multiple of 10 sts plus 5.

38

Multiple of 8 sts plus 1.

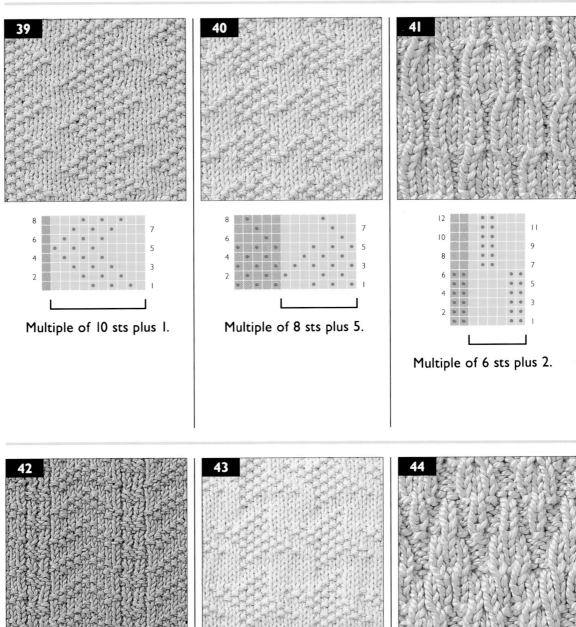

Multiple of 10 sts plus 1.

Multiple of 8 sts plus 5.

Multiple of 6 sts plus 2.

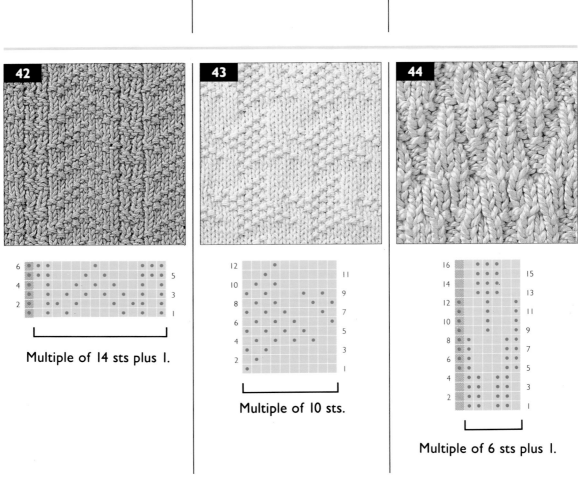

Multiple of 14 sts plus 1.

Multiple of 10 sts.

Multiple of 6 sts plus 1.

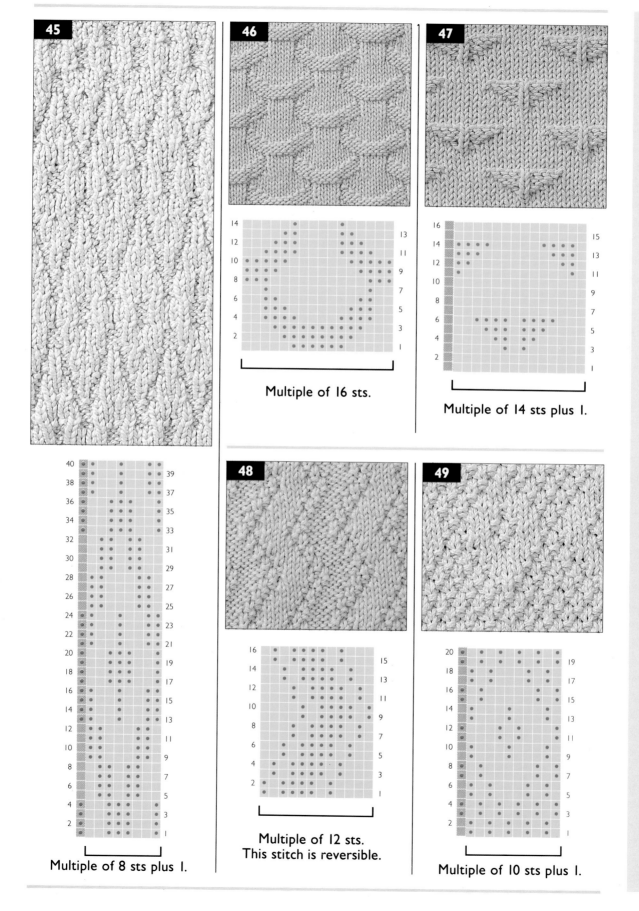

45

46

Multiple of 16 sts.

47

Multiple of 14 sts plus 1.

Multiple of 8 sts plus 1.

48

Multiple of 12 sts.
This stitch is reversible.

49

Multiple of 10 sts plus 1.

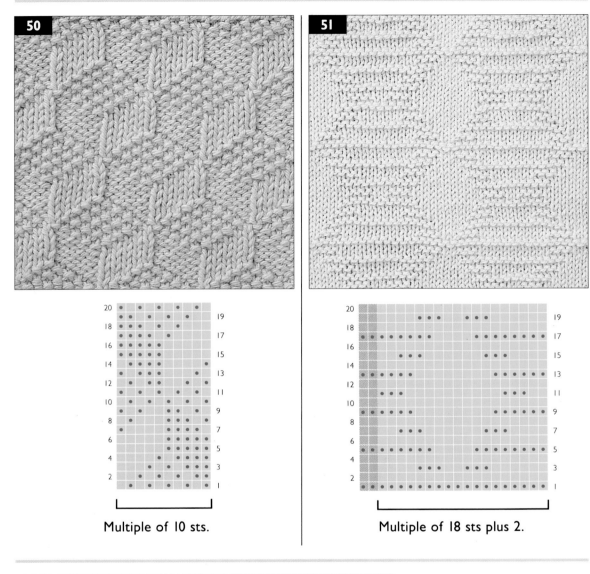

50

Multiple of 10 sts.

51

Multiple of 18 sts plus 2.

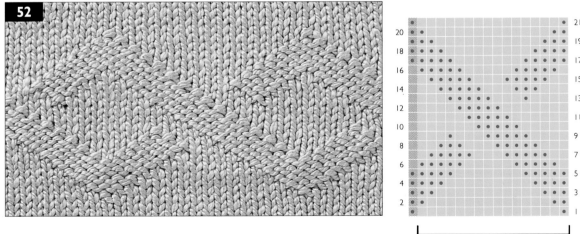

52

Multiple of 16 sts plus 1.

53

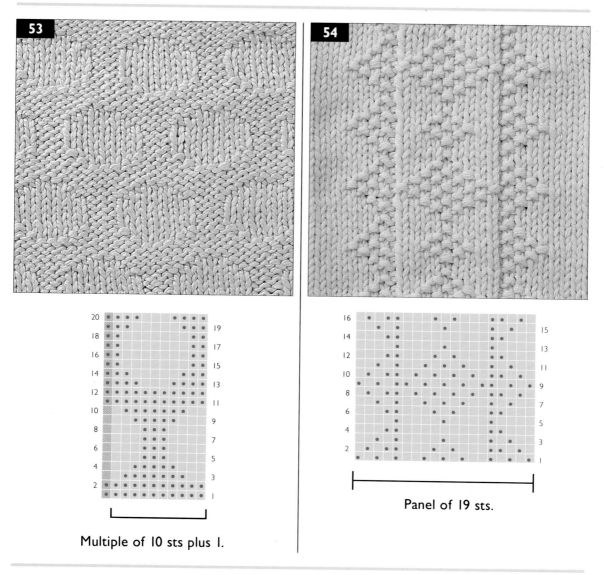

Multiple of 10 sts plus 1.

54

Panel of 19 sts.

55

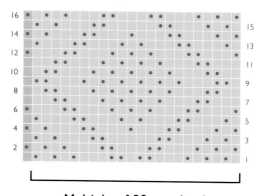

Multiple of 22 sts plus 1.

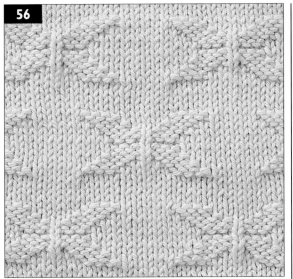

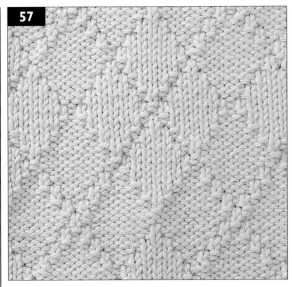

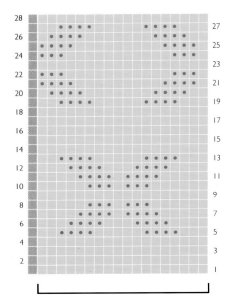

Multiple of 18 sts plus 1.

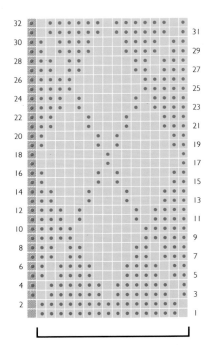

Multiple of 16 sts plus 1.

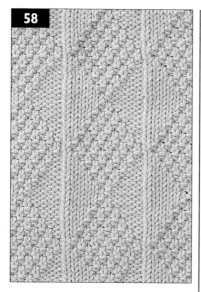

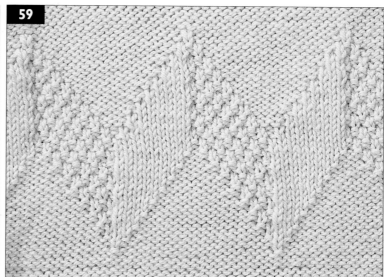

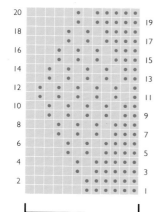

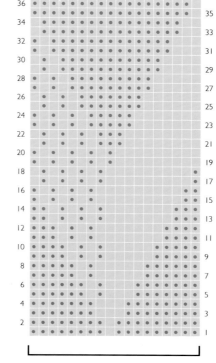

Multiple of 12 sts.
This stitch is reversible.

Multiple of 18 sts.

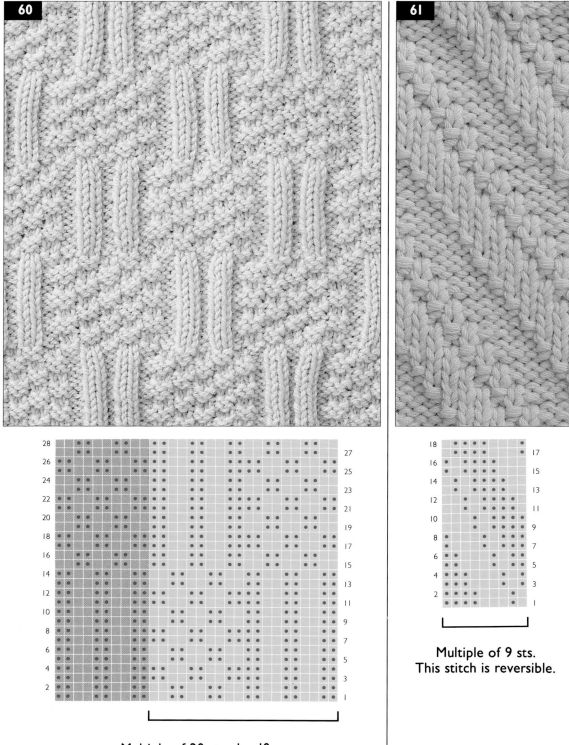

60

61

Multiple of 20 sts plus 10.

Multiple of 9 sts.
This stitch is reversible.

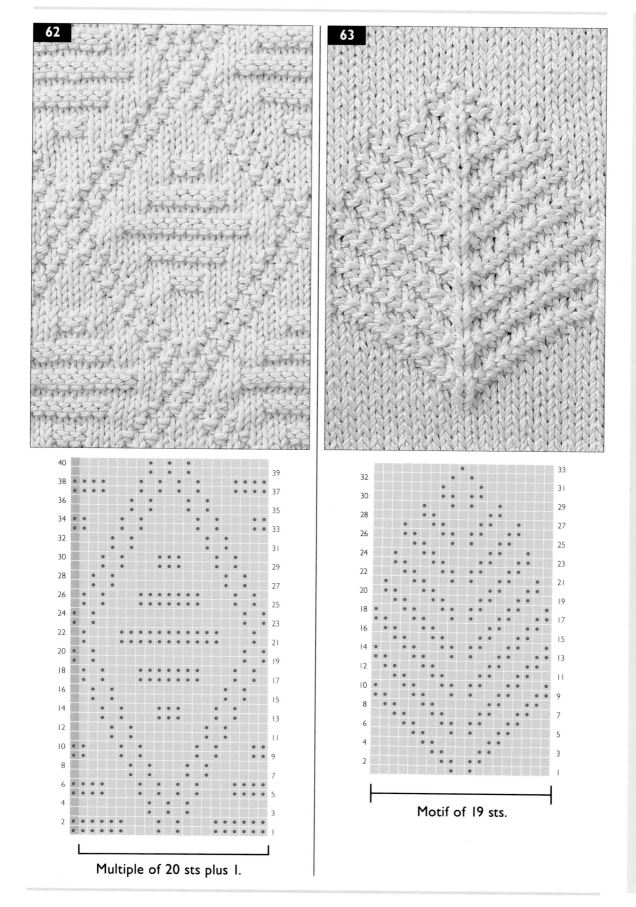

62

63

Multiple of 20 sts plus 1.

Motif of 19 sts.

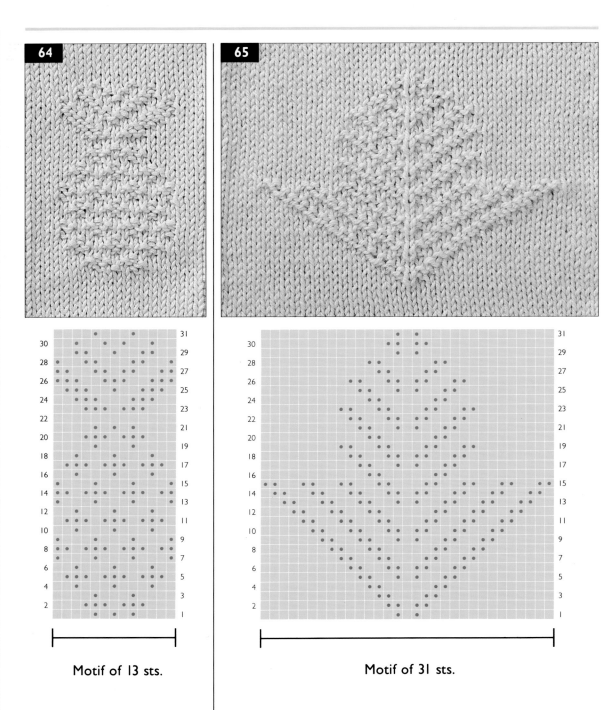

Motif of 13 sts.

Motif of 31 sts.

66

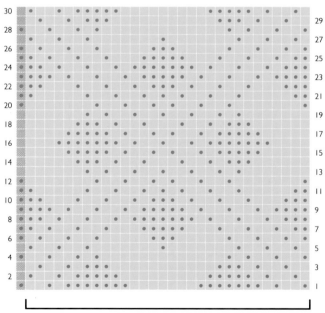

Multiple of 30 sts plus 1.

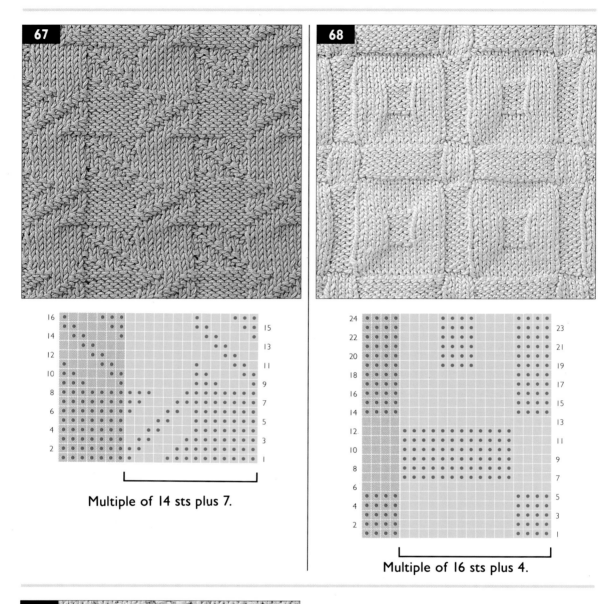

67

Multiple of 14 sts plus 7.

68

Multiple of 16 sts plus 4.

69

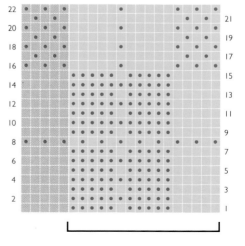

Multiple of 16 sts plus 5.

70

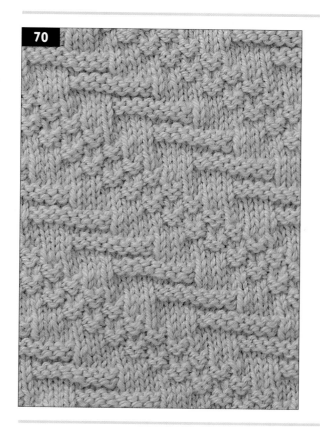

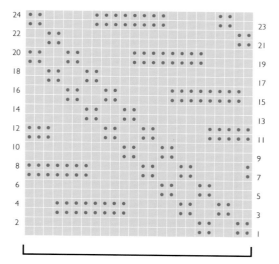

Multiple of 24 sts.

71

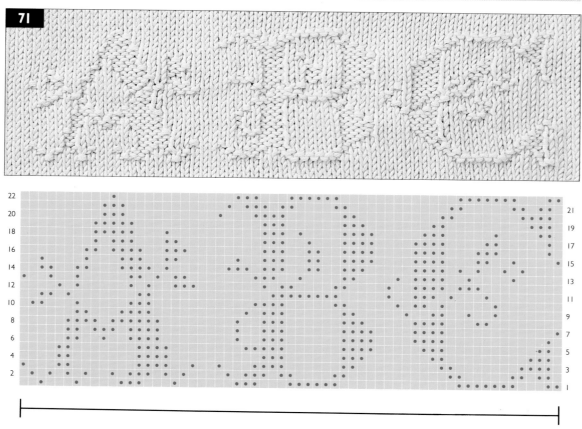

Motif of 61 sts.

Multiple of 54 sts plus 1.

CABLE STITCHES

Cables are stitches that look like twisted ropes, interwoven plaits and criss-cross trellises and which seem so complicated to the uninitiated. But the principle is simple: making a cable is merely working stitches, or groups of stitches, out of sequence. A cable needle (a short, double-pointed needle, usually curved or notched) is used to hold the first stitch(es) to the front or back while working the following stitch(es); the knitting is then resumed from the cable needle. Cables are usually worked in stockinette stitch on a plain or textured ground, but they look particularly rich when they themselves are textured.

Besides raising the surface, cables contract the knitted fabric, so it's usually a good idea to work increases into the base of a cable panel or motif and decreases into the top to prevent flaring above and below. The density of the fabric makes cables ideal for outdoor wear.

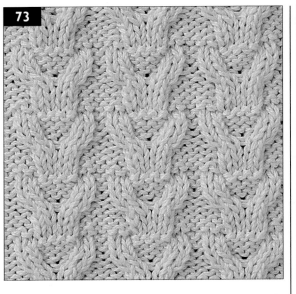

73

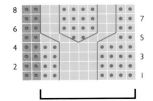

Multiple of 10 sts plus 2.

74

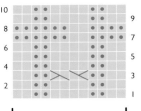

Multiple of 12 sts.

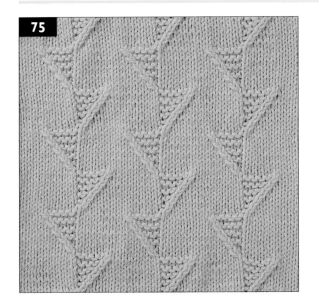

75

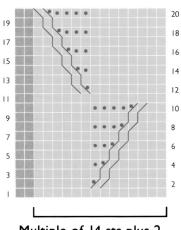

Multiple of 14 sts plus 2.

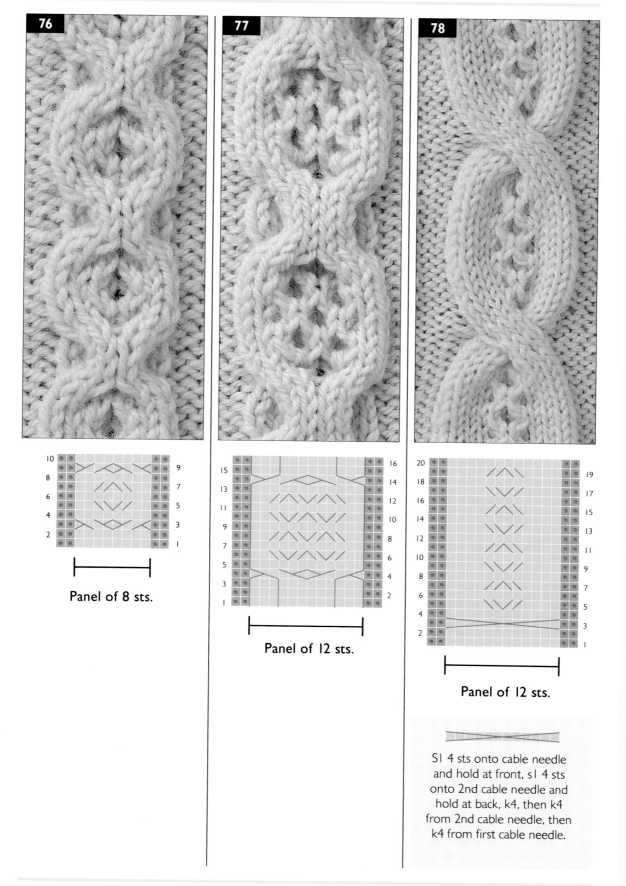

76

77

78

10
8
6
4
2
9
7
5
3
1

Panel of 8 sts.

15
13
11
9
7
5
3
1
16
14
12
10
8
6
4
2

Panel of 12 sts.

20
18
16
14
12
10
8
6
4
2
19
17
15
13
11
9
7
5
3
1

Panel of 12 sts.

Sl 4 sts onto cable needle
and hold at front, sl 4 sts
onto 2nd cable needle and
hold at back, k4, then k4
from 2nd cable needle, then
k4 from first cable needle.

53

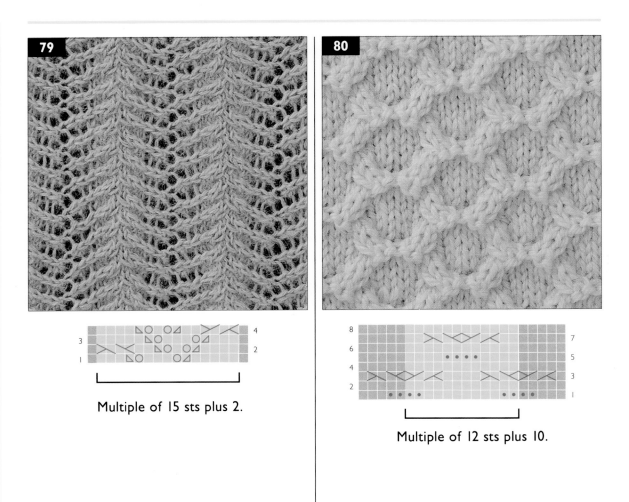

79

Multiple of 15 sts plus 2.

80

Multiple of 12 sts plus 10.

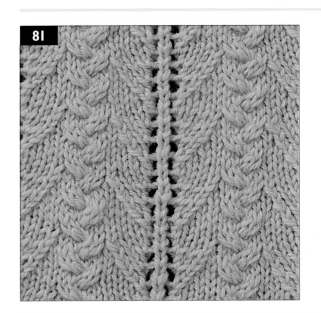

81

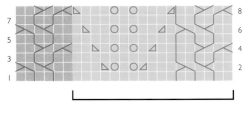

Multiple of 17 sts plus 6.

82

83

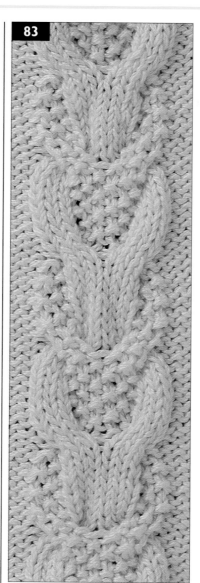

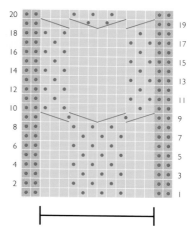

Panel of 12 sts.

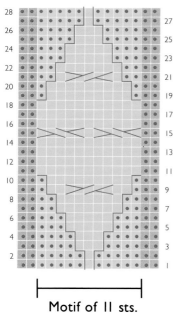

Motif of 11 sts.

Sl 3 sts onto cable needle and hold at back, k2, then k3 sts from cable needle.

Sl 2 sts onto cable needle and hold at front, k3 then k2 sts from cable needle.

Sl 3 sts onto cable needle and hold at back, pl, kl, pl, then k3 from cable needle.

Sl 3 sts onto cable needle and hold at front, k3, then kl, pl, kl from cable needle.

Sl 3 sts onto cable needle and hold at back, k3, then pl, kl, pl from cable needle.

Sl 3 sts onto cable needle and hold at front, kl, pl, kl, then k3 sts from cable needle.

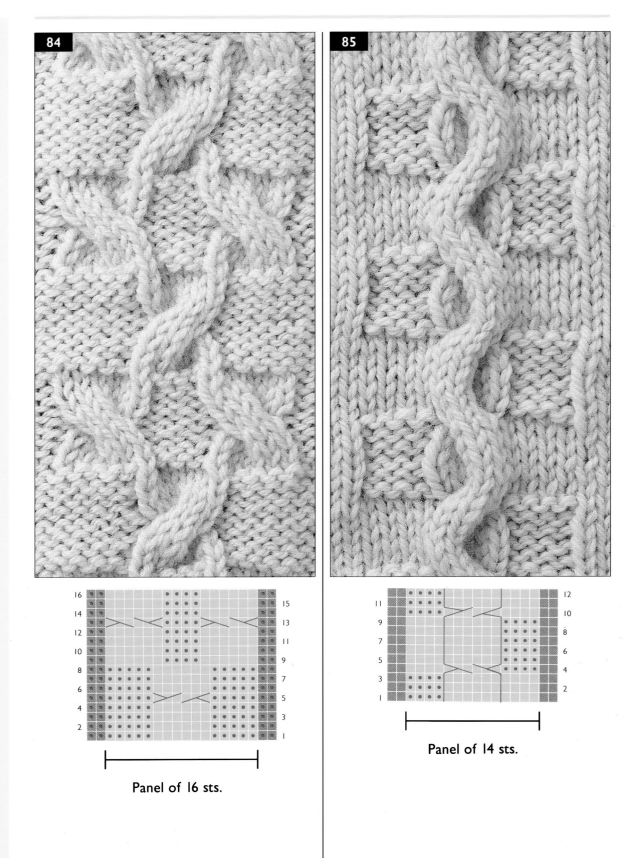

84

85

Panel of 16 sts.

Panel of 14 sts.

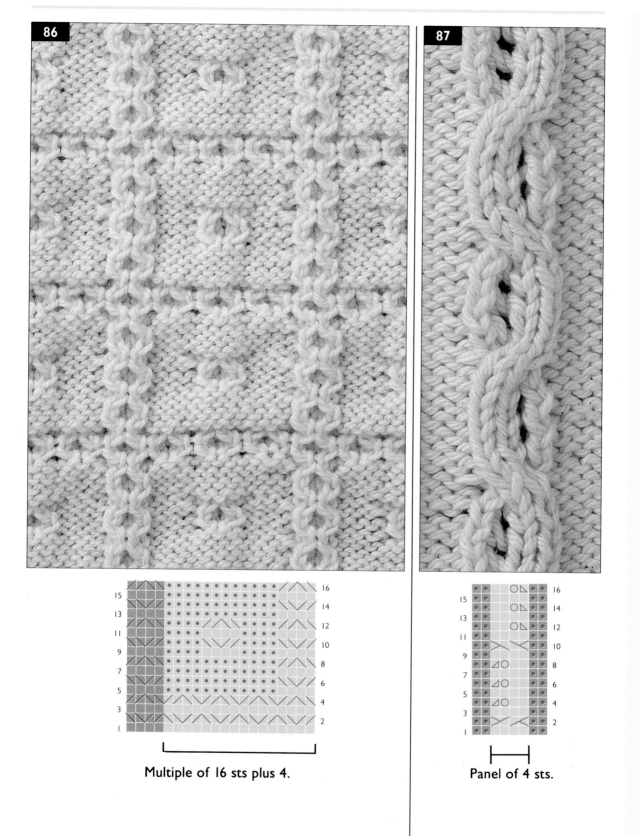

86

87

Multiple of 16 sts plus 4.

Panel of 4 sts.

88

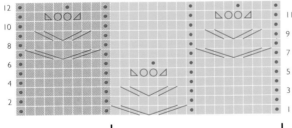

Multiple of 18 sts plus 10.

Sl 3 sts onto cable needle
and hold at back, k1, then k3
sts from cable needle, sl 1 st
onto cable needle and hold
at front, k3, then k1 st from
cable needle.

89

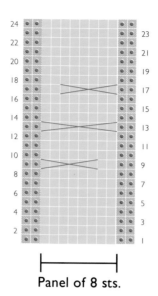

Panel of 8 sts.

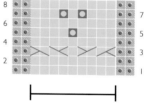

Sl 2 sts onto cable needle and hold at front, k4, then k2 from cable needle.

Sl 2 sts onto cable needle and hold at front, k6, then k2 from cable needle.

90

Panel of 9 sts.

CABLE STITCHES

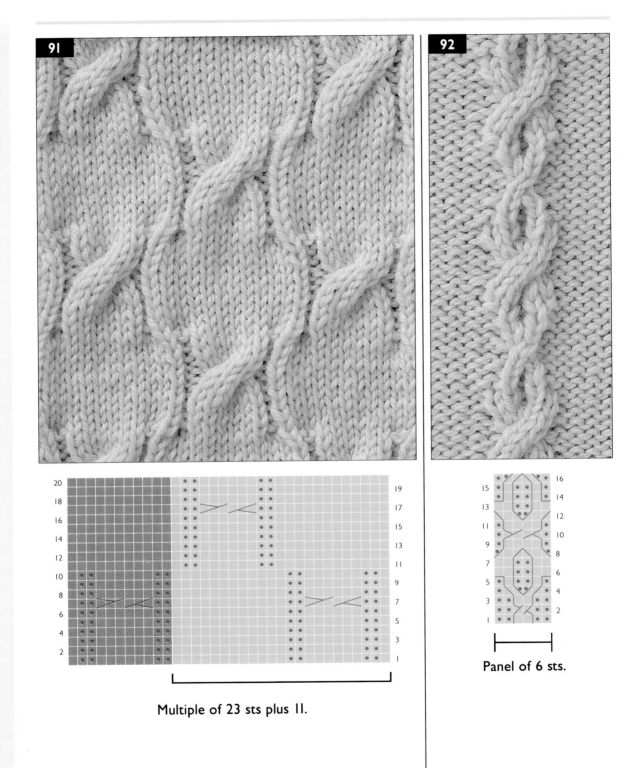

Multiple of 23 sts plus 11.

Panel of 6 sts.

60

93

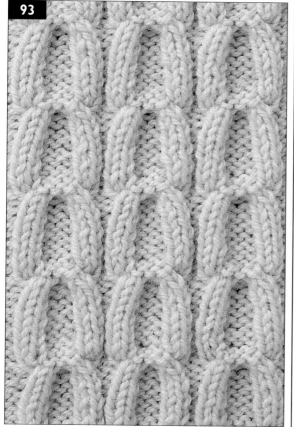

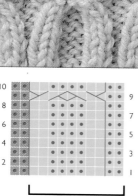

Multiple of 10 sts plus 2.

Sl next 2 sts onto cable needle and hold at front, k2, then p2 from cable needle.

Sl next 2 sts onto cable needle and hold at back, p2, then k2 from cable needle.

94

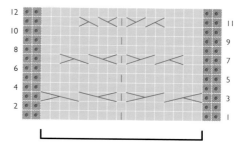

Panel of 17 sts.

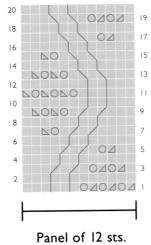

Panel of 12 sts.

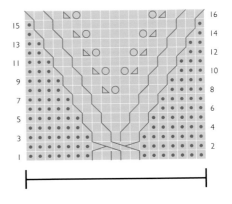

Panel of 19 sts.

97

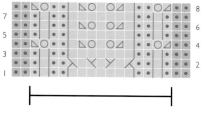

Panel of 15 sts.

98

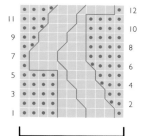

Multiple of 11 sts.

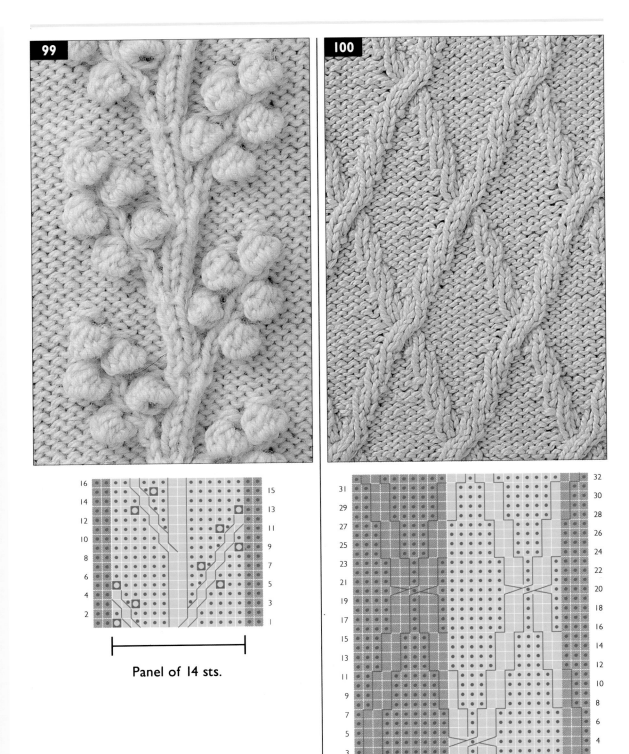

Panel of 14 sts.

Multiple of 12 sts plus 13.

101

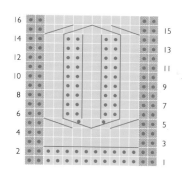

Panel of 10 sts.

Sl 3 sts onto cable needle
and hold at back, k2, then
p2, k1 from cable needle.

Sl 2 sts onto cable needle
and hold at front, k1, p2,
then k2 from cable needle.

Sl 2 sts onto cable needle
and hold at front, k3, then
k2 from cable needle.

Sl 3 sts onto cable needle
and hold at back, k2, then k3
from cable needle.

102

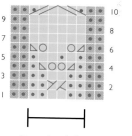

Panel of 6 sts.

103

104

105

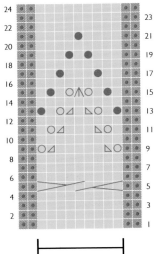

Panel of 9 sts.

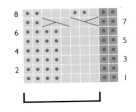

Multiple of 8 sts plus 2.

Sl 3 sts onto cable needle
and hold at front, k1, p2,
then k3 from cable needle.

Panel of 12 sts.

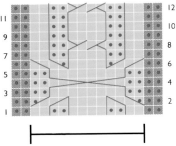

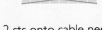

Sl 2 sts onto cable needle
and hold at front, sl next 4
sts onto 2nd cable needle
and hold at back, k2, then k4
from 2nd cable needle, then
k2 from first cable needle.

106

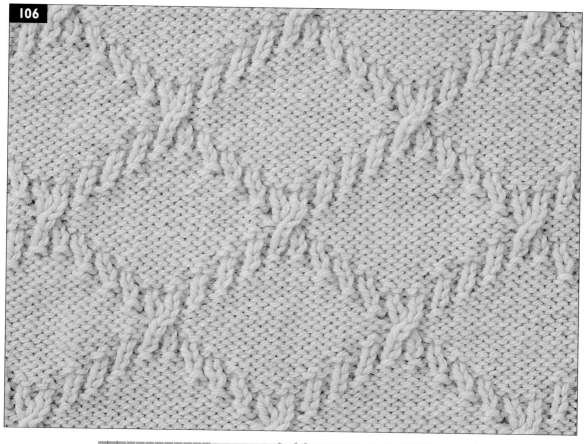

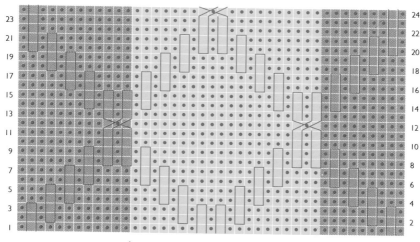

Multiple of 20 sts plus 21.

107

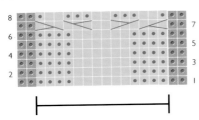

Panel of 14 sts.

Sl next 3 sts onto cable needle and hold at back, p1, k2, then p3 sts from cable needle.

Sl next 3 sts onto cable needle and hold at front, p3, then k2, p1 from cable needle.

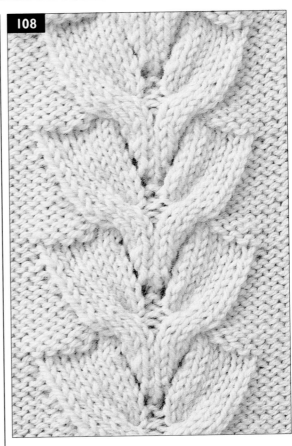

108

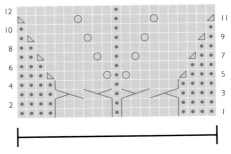

Panel of 21 sts.

109

110

Panel of 18 sts.

Multiple of 18 sts.

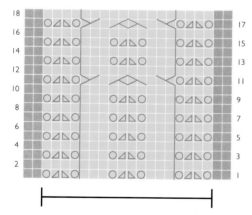

Sl 3 sts onto cable needle
and hold at front, k2, then
k3 from cable needle.

Sl 2 sts onto cable needle
and hold at back, k3, then k2
sts from cable needle.

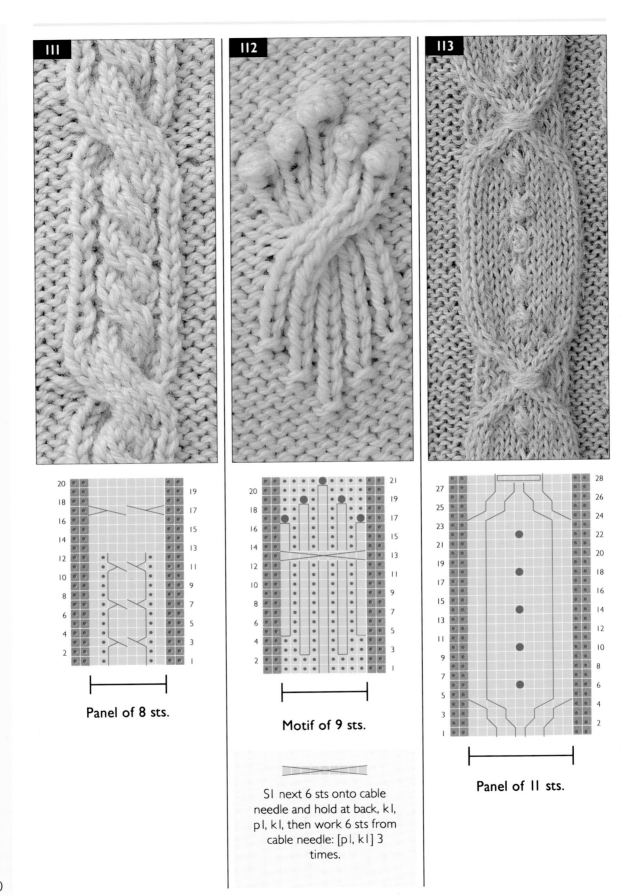

Panel of 8 sts.

Motif of 9 sts.

Panel of 11 sts.

Sl next 6 sts onto cable needle and hold at back, k1, p1, k1, then work 6 sts from cable needle: [p1, k1] 3 times.

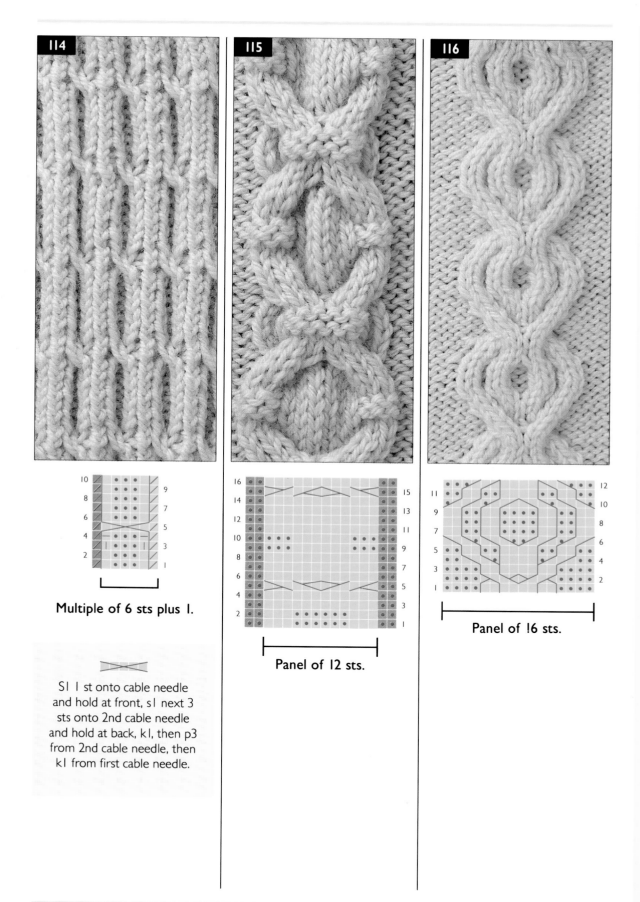

114

115

116

Multiple of 6 sts plus 1.

Panel of 12 sts.

Panel of 16 sts.

Sl 1 st onto cable needle and hold at front, sl next 3 sts onto 2nd cable needle and hold at back, k1, then p3 from 2nd cable needle, then k1 from first cable needle.

117

118

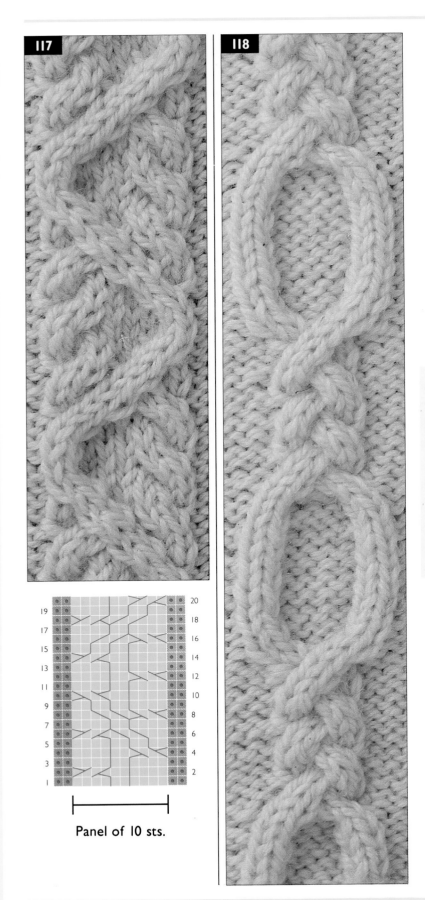

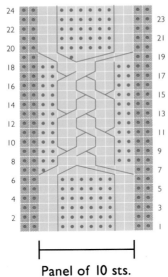

Panel of 10 sts.

Sl next 2 sts onto cable needle and hold at front, p2, k2, then k2 from cable needle.

Sl next 4 sts onto cable needle and hold at back, k2, then p4 sts from cable needle.

Panel of 10 sts.

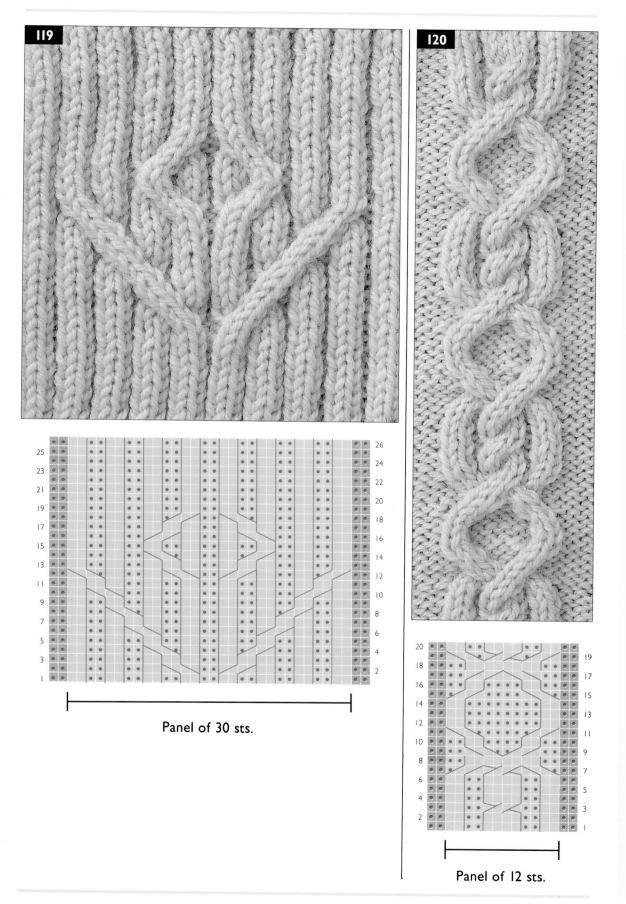

119

Panel of 30 sts.

120

Panel of 12 sts.

121

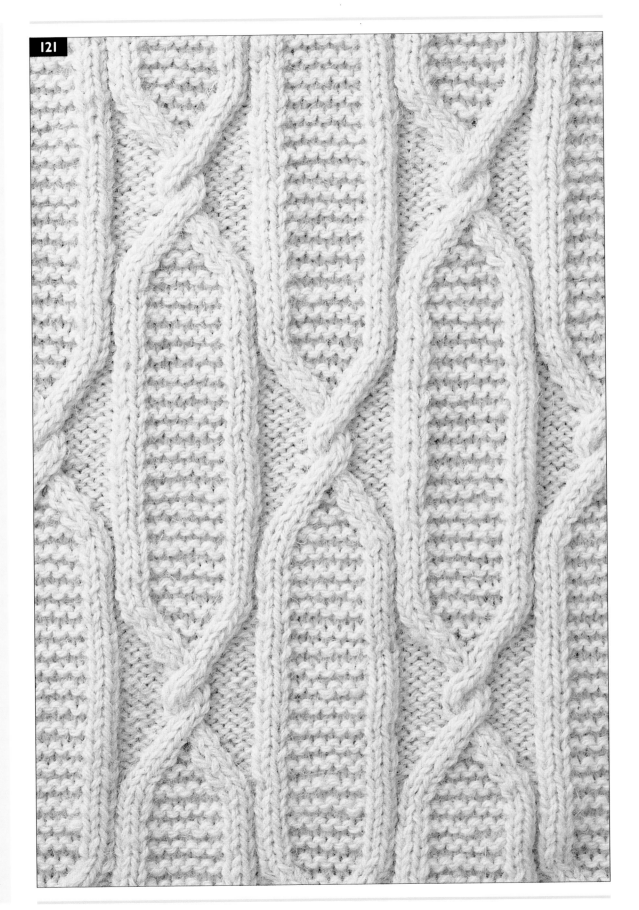

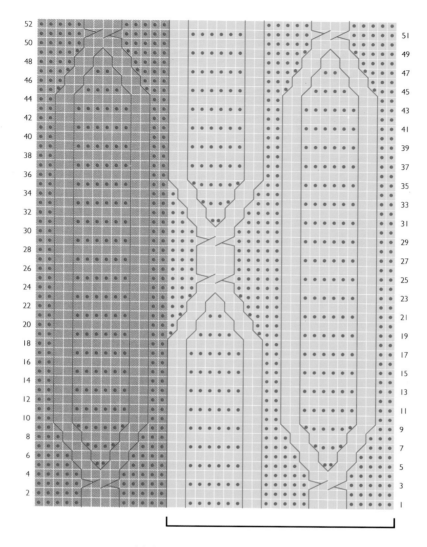

Multiple of 24 sts plus 14.

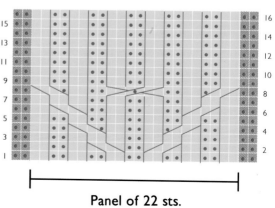

Panel of 22 sts.

123

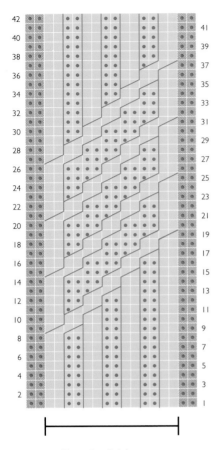

Panel of 14 sts.

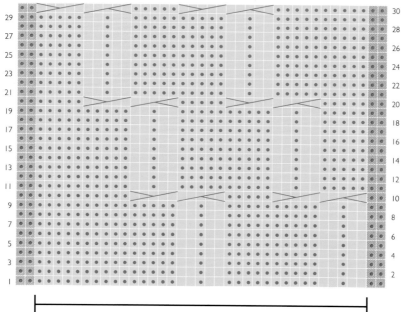

Panel of 35 sts.

Sl next 5 sts onto cable needle and hold at back, p5, then work k2, p1, k2 from cable needle.

125

126

32		31
30		29
28		27
26		25
24		23
22		21
20		19
18		17
16		15
14		13
12		11
10		9
8		7
6		5
4		3
2		1

Multiple of 12 sts plus 4.

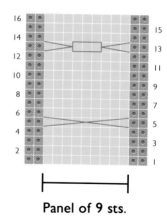

Panel of 9 sts.

SI 6 sts onto cable needle
and hold at back, k3, sl last 3
sts from cable needle back
onto left-hand needle, k3,
then k3 sts from cable
needle.

SI 3 sts onto first cable
needle and hold at back, sl
next 3 sts onto 2nd cable
needle and hold at front, k3,
k3 from 2nd cable needle,
k3 from first cable needle.

127

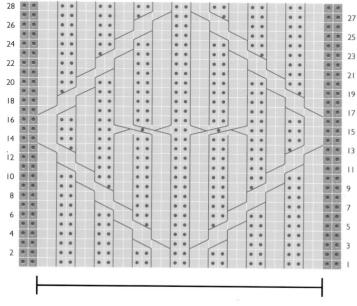

Panel of 30 sts.

128

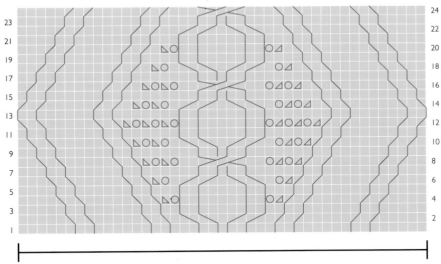

Panel of 43 sts.

129

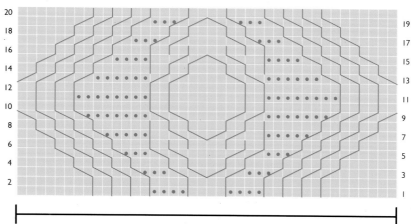

Panel of 40 sts.

130

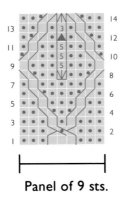

Panel of 9 sts.

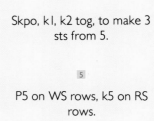

Skpo, k1, k2 tog, to make 3 sts from 5.

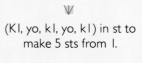

P5 on WS rows, k5 on RS rows.

(K1, yo, k1, yo, k1) in st to make 5 sts from 1.

P3.

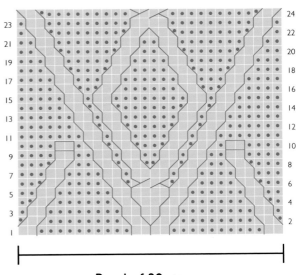

Panel of 28 sts.

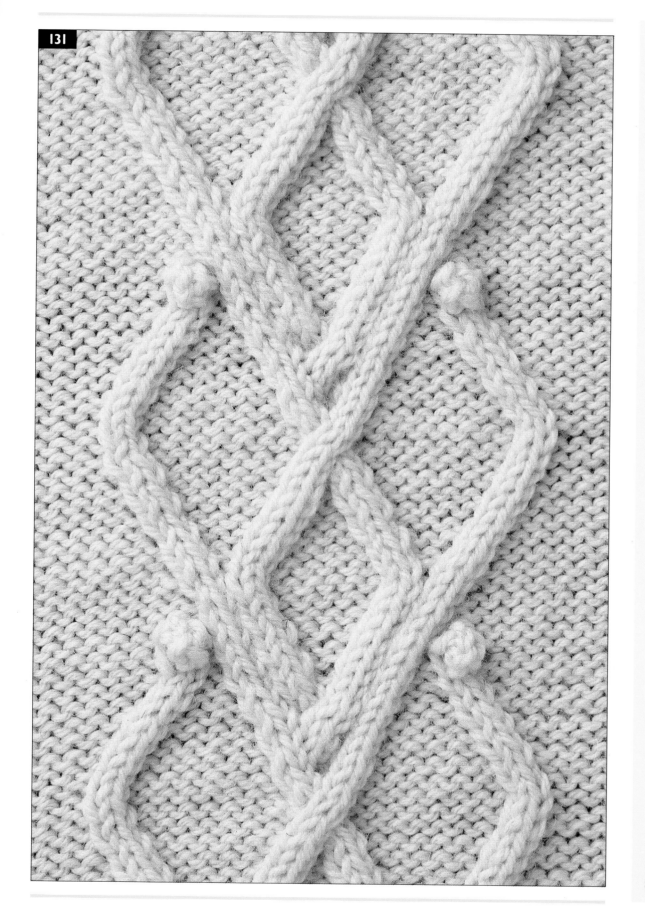

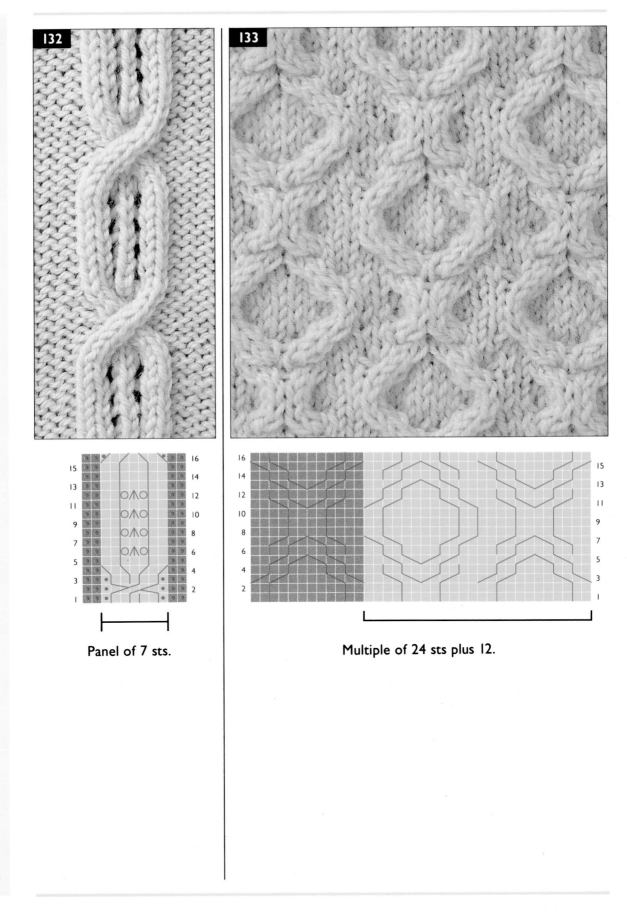

132

15
13
11
9
7
5
3
1

16
14
12
10
8
6
4
2

Panel of 7 sts.

133

16
14
12
10
8
6
4
2

15
13
11
9
7
5
3
1

Multiple of 24 sts plus 12.

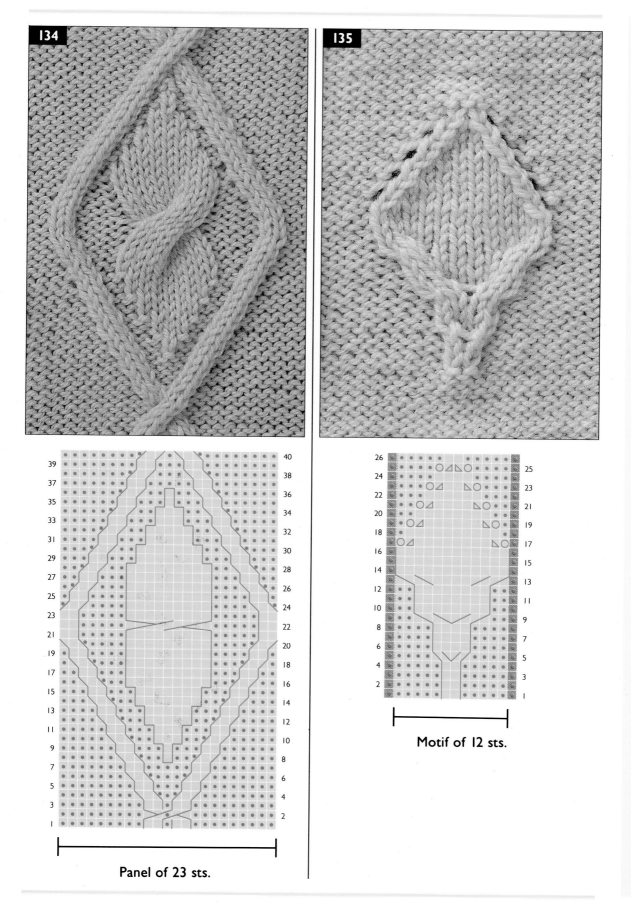

134

135

Panel of 23 sts.

Motif of 12 sts.

136

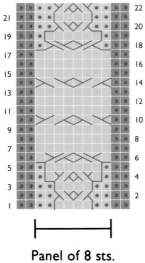

Panel of 8 sts.

137

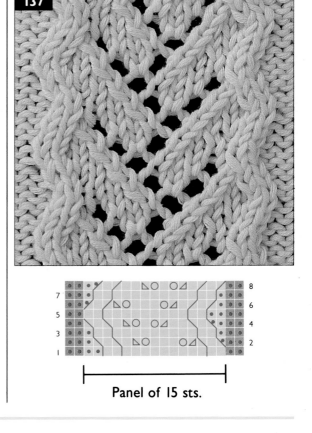

Panel of 15 sts.

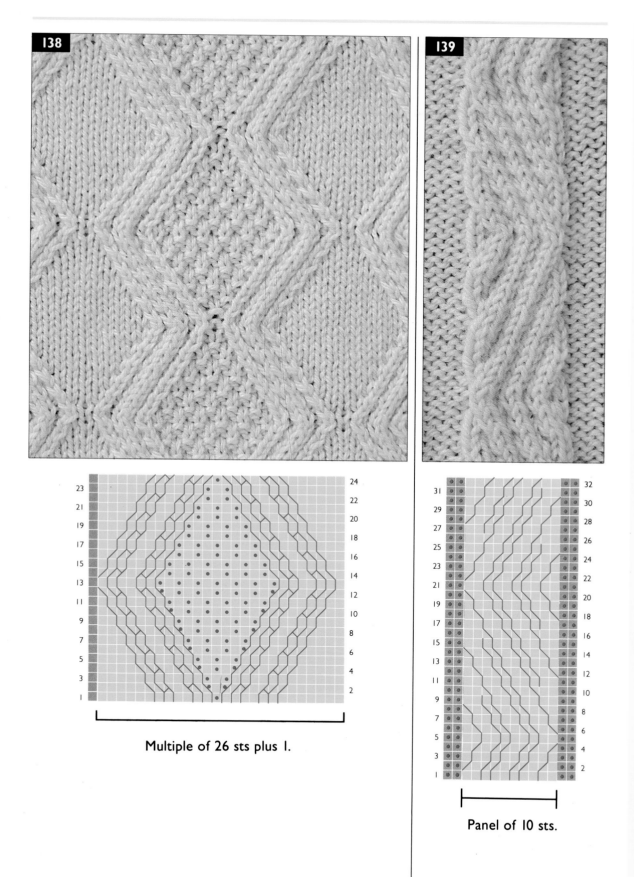

138

Multiple of 26 sts plus 1.

139

Panel of 10 sts.

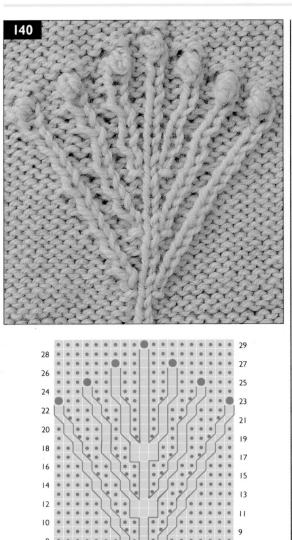

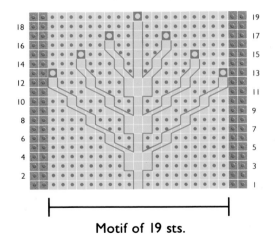

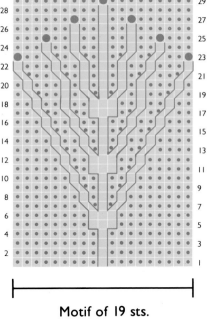

Motif of 19 sts.

Motif of 19 sts.

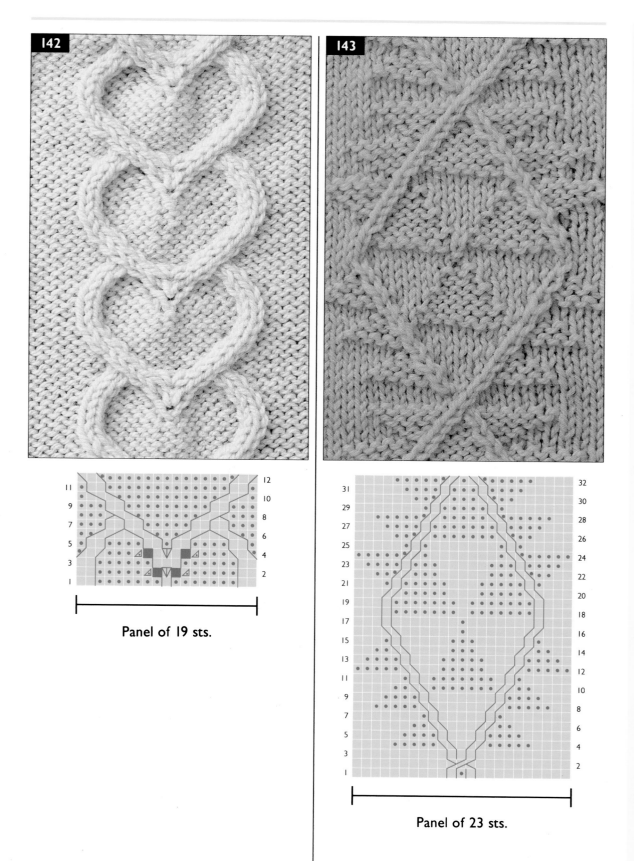

142

143

Panel of 19 sts.

Panel of 23 sts.

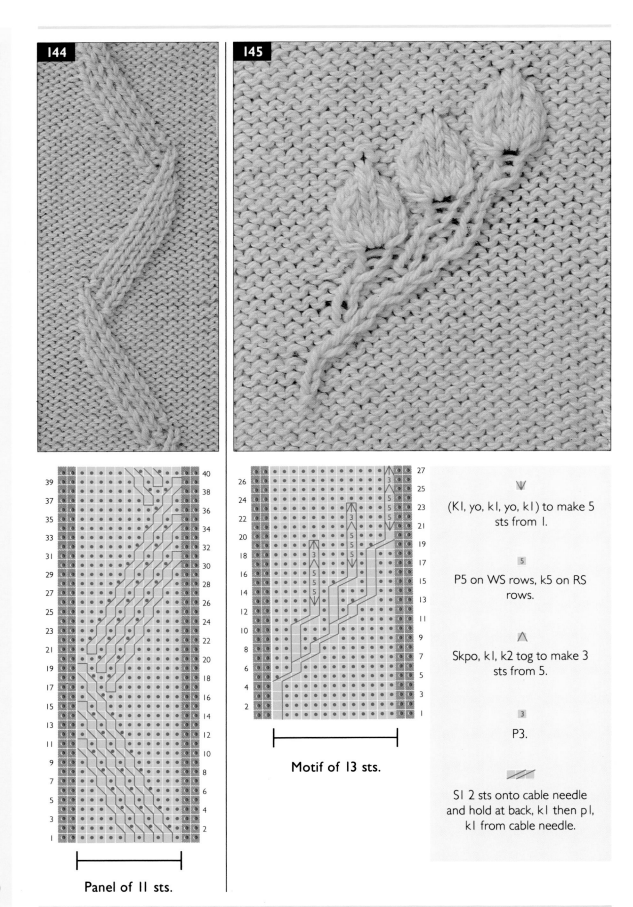

144

145

Panel of 11 sts.

Motif of 13 sts.

ᴗ

(K1, yo, k1, yo, k1) to make 5 sts from 1.

5

P5 on WS rows, k5 on RS rows.

ᴧ

Skpo, k1, k2 tog to make 3 sts from 5.

3

P3.

Sl 2 sts onto cable needle and hold at back, k1 then p1, k1 from cable needle.

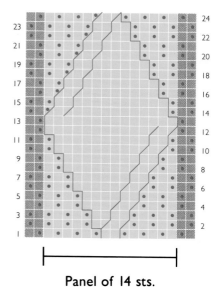

Panel of 14 sts.

146

147

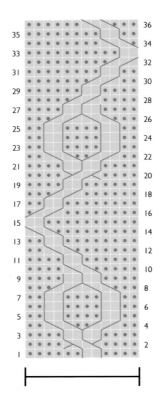

Panel of 12 sts.

148

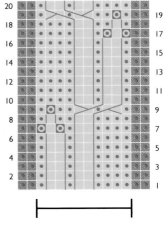

Panel of 10 sts.

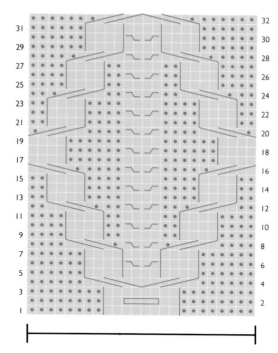

Panel of 24 sts.

Sl 4 sts onto cable needle and hold at back, k2, then k4 from cable needle.

Sl 2 sts onto cable needle and hold at front, k4, then k2 from cable needle.

Sl 4 sts onto cable needle and hold at back, k2, then work k2, p2 from cable needle.

Sl 2 sts onto cable needle and hold at front, p2, k2, then k2 from cable needle.

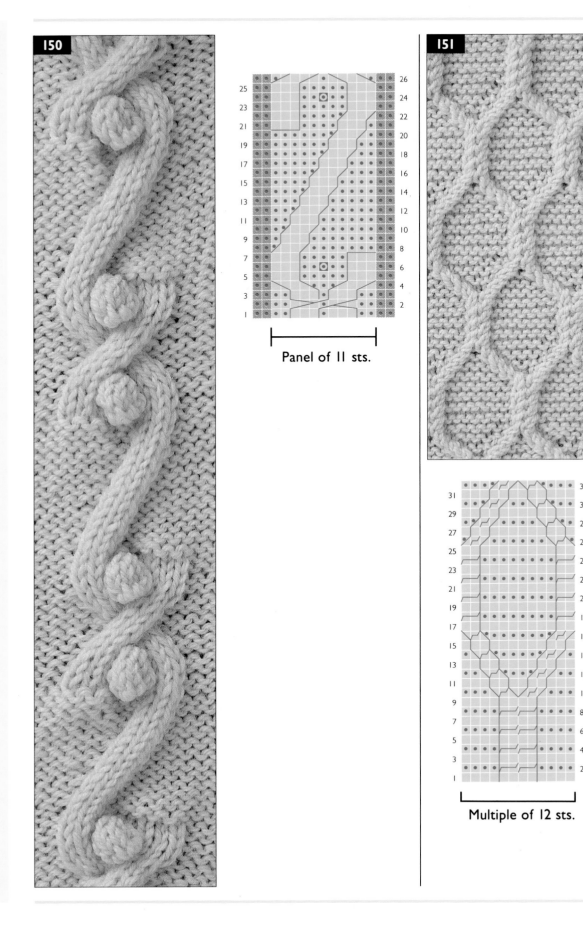

150

151

Panel of 11 sts.

Multiple of 12 sts.

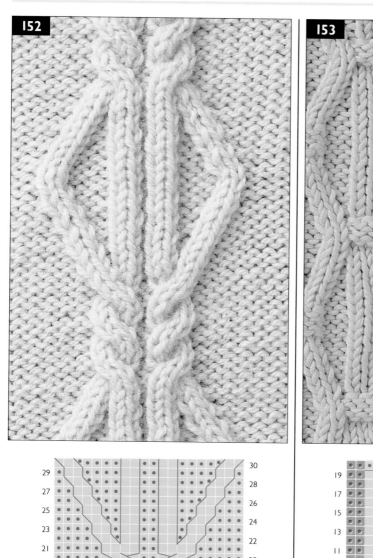

152

153

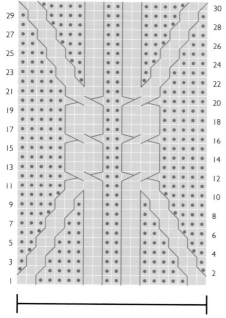

Panel of 20 sts.

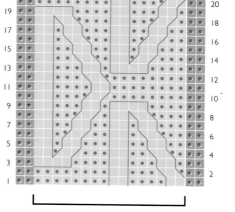

Multiple of 16 sts plus 4.

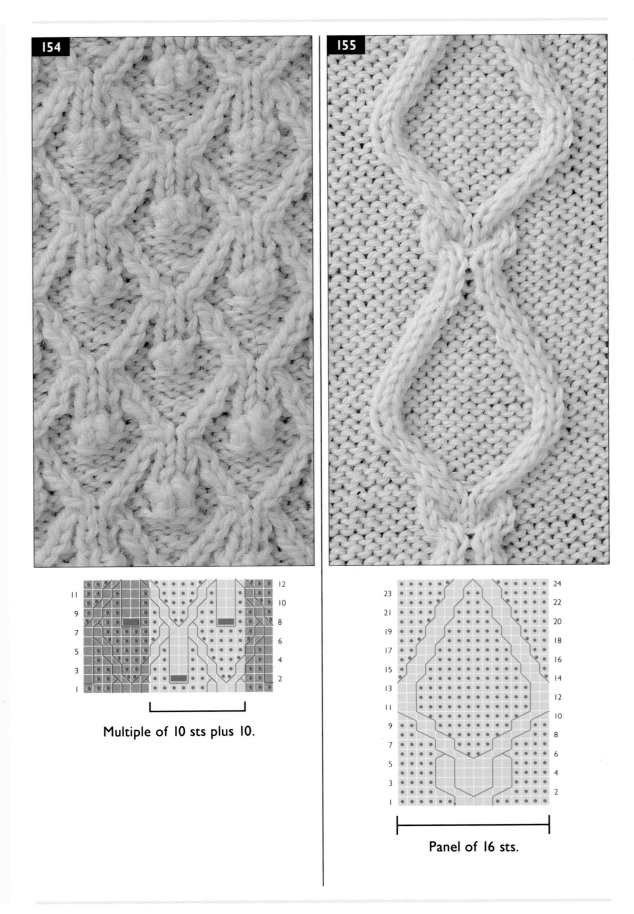

154

Multiple of 10 sts plus 10.

155

Panel of 16 sts.

156

157

Panel of 20 sts.

Panel of 16 sts.

158

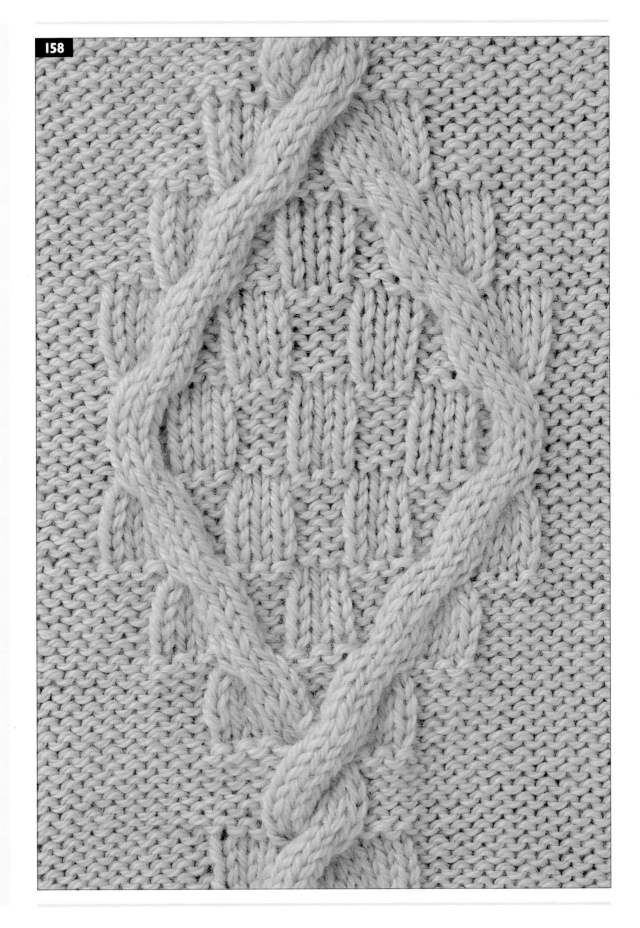

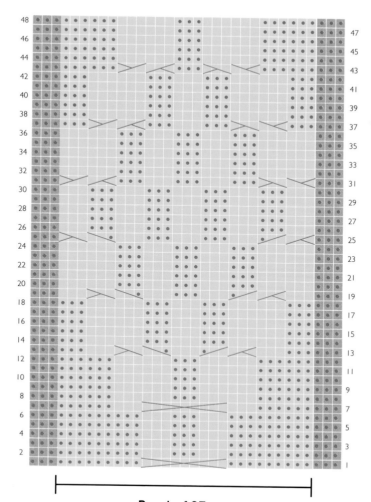

Panel of 27 sts.

159

Sl next 3 sts onto cable needle and hold at back, k3, then p3 from cable needle.

Sl next 3 sts onto cable needle and hold at front, p3, then k3 from cable needle.

Sl next 6 sts onto cable needle and hold at back, k3, sl last 3 sts from cable needle to left-hand needle, p3, then k3 remaining sts from cable needle.

Panel of 5 sts.
All k sts of cables are worked tbl.

160

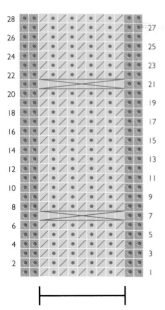

Panel of 9 sts.

Sl 3 sts onto first cable needle and hold at back, sl next 3 sts onto 2nd cable needle and hold at front, k1 tbl, p1, k1 tbl, then work sts from 2nd cable needle p1, k1 tbl, p1, then work sts from first cable needle k1 tbl, p1, k1 tbl.

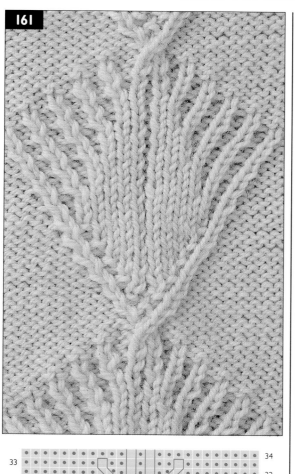

161

162

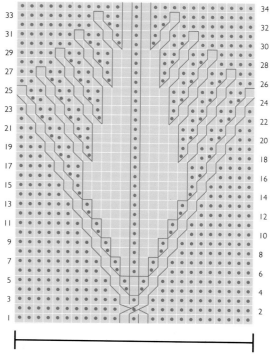

Panel of 25 sts.

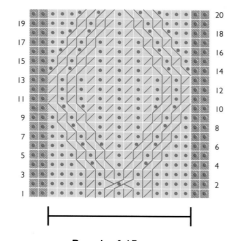

Panel of 15 sts.
All k sts of cables are worked tbl.

163

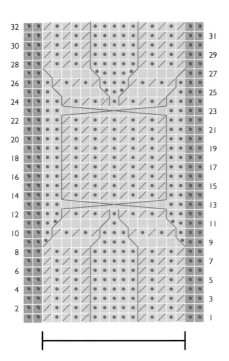

Panel of 15 sts.

SI 1 st onto cable needle and hold at back, k1 tbl, [p1, k1 tbl] twice, then p1 st from cable needle.

SI 5 sts onto cable needle and hold at front, p1, then work k1 tbl, [p1, k1 tbl] twice from cable needle.

SI 6 sts onto cable needle and hold at back, k1 tbl, [p1, k1 tbl] twice, then work sts from cable needle [p1, k1 tbl] 3 times.

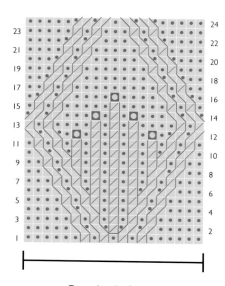

Panel of 19 sts.
All k sts of cables are worked tbl.

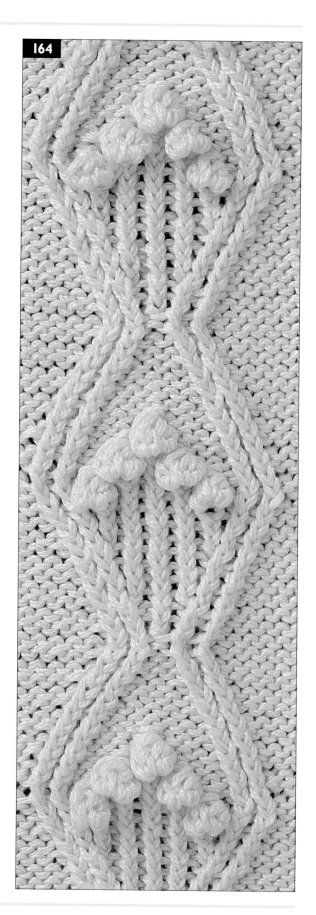

164

165

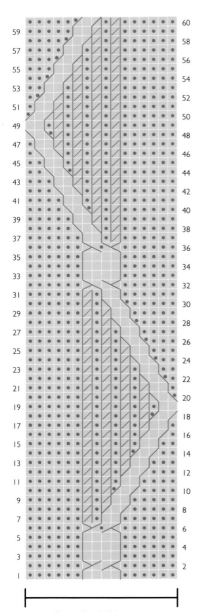

Panel of 16 sts.

S1 2 sts onto cable needle
and hold at back, k2, then
p1, k1 tbl from cable needle.

S1 2 sts onto cable needle
and hold at front, k1 tbl, p1
then k 2 sts from cable
needle.

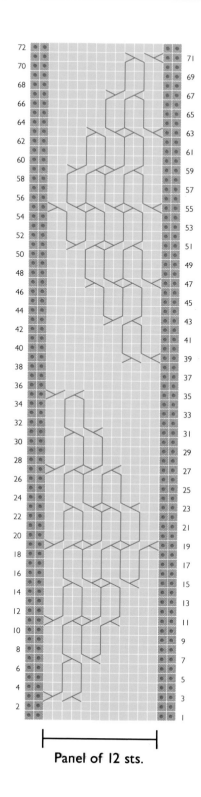

Panel of 12 sts.

166

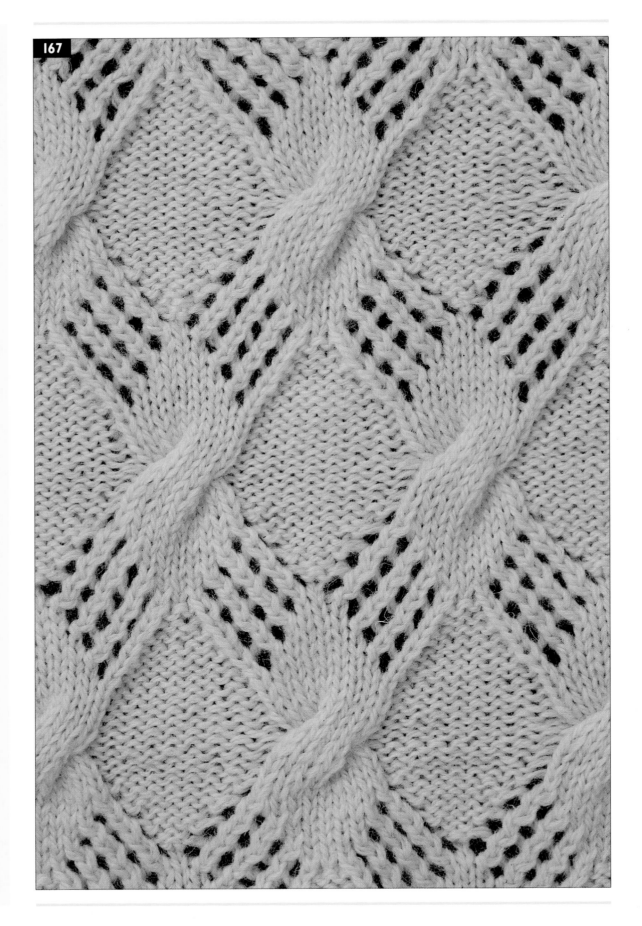

168

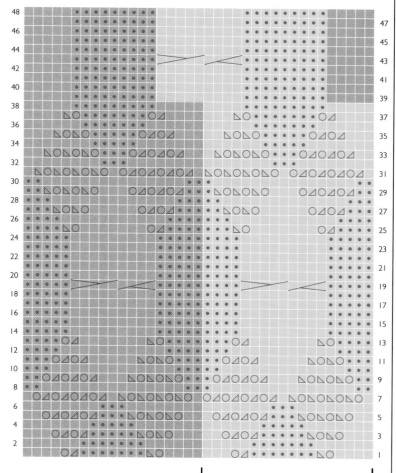

Multiple of 18 sts plus 19.

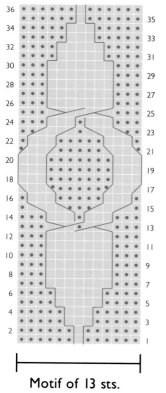

Motif of 13 sts.

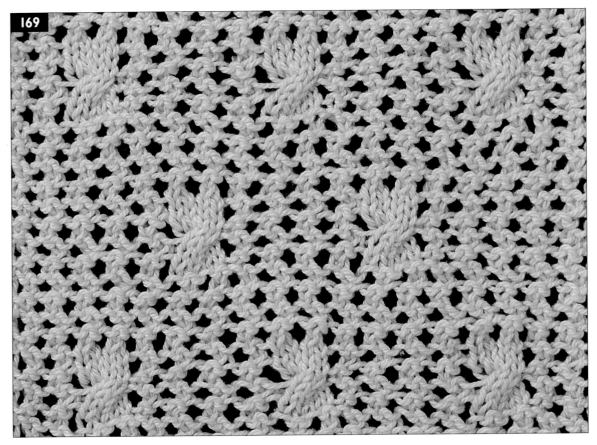

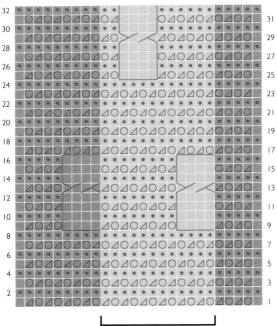

Multiple of 12 sts plus 14.

170

171

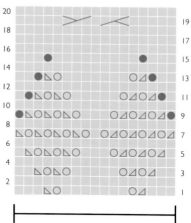

Panel of 17 sts.

Sl next 3 sts onto cable
needle and hold at back, k4,
then k3 from cable needle.

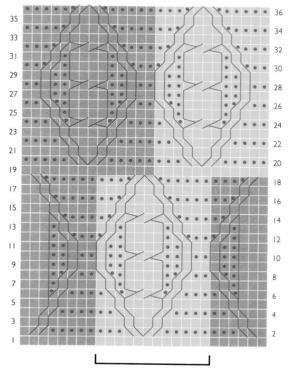

Multiple of 12 sts plus 14.

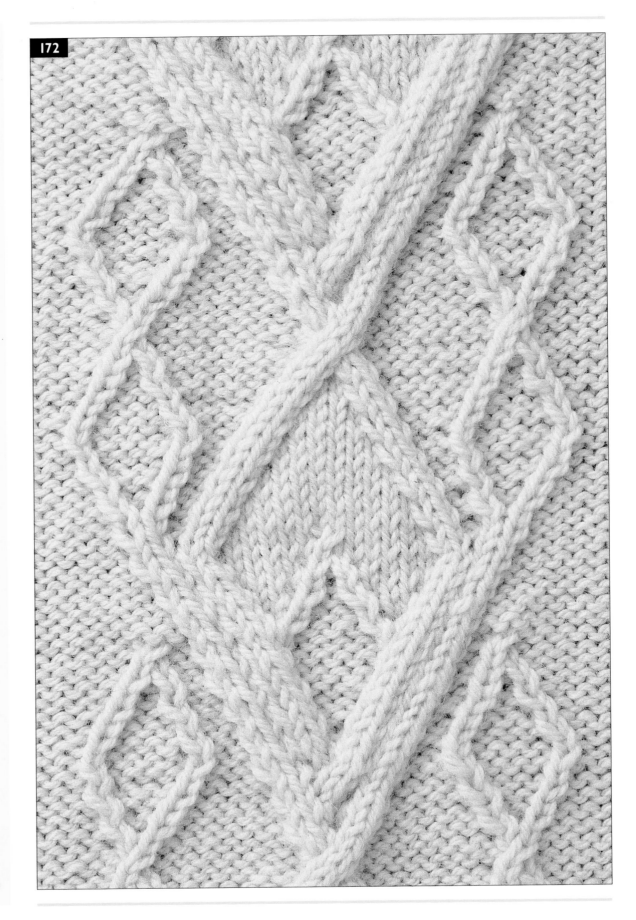

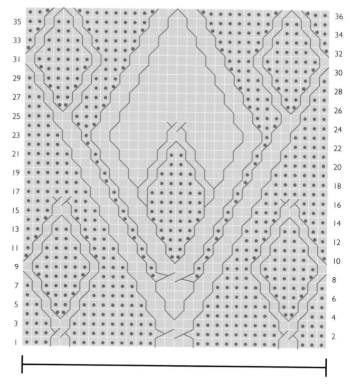

Panel of 32 sts.

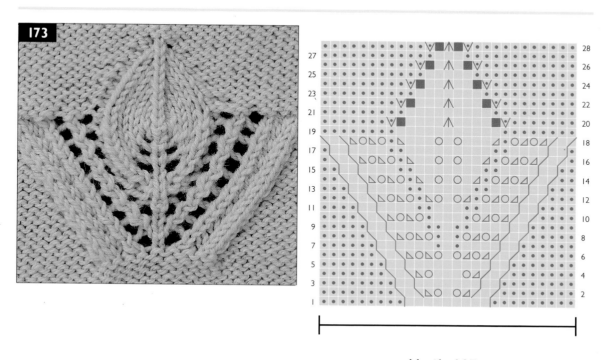

173

Motif of 27 sts.

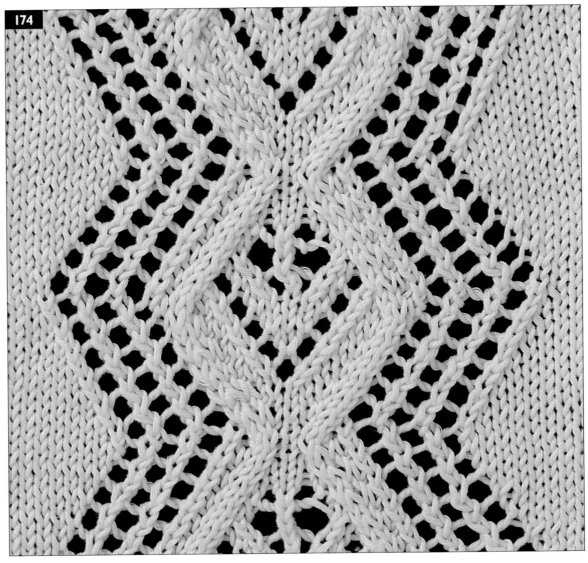

174

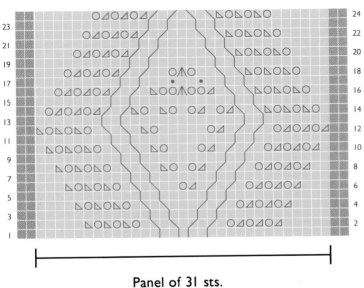

Panel of 31 sts.

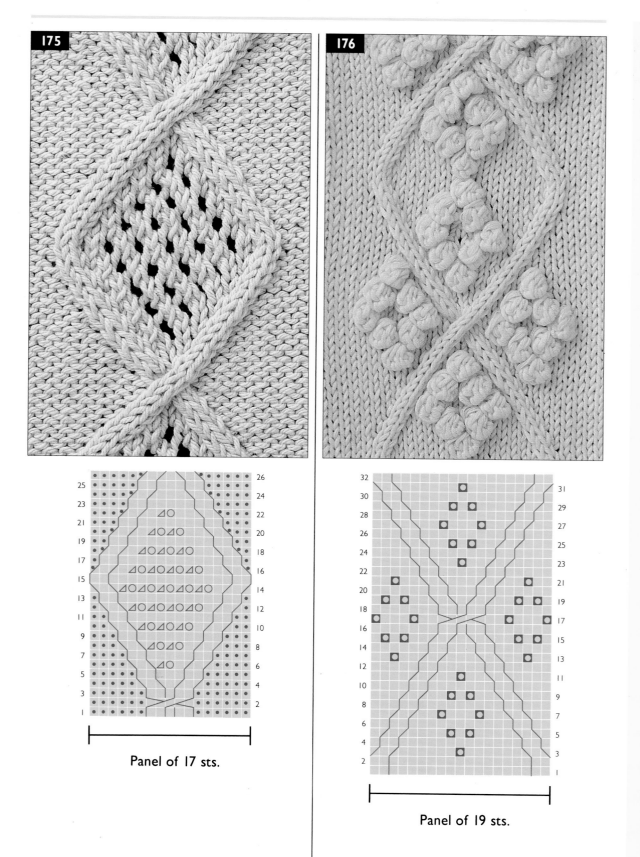

175

176

Panel of 17 sts.

Panel of 19 sts.

177

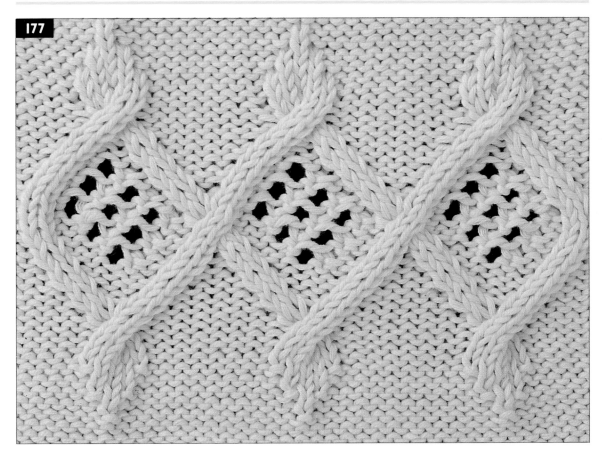

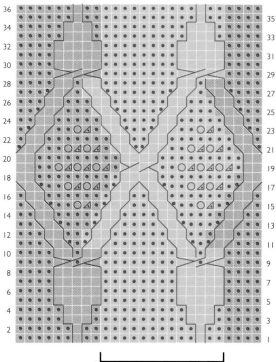

Multiple of 13 sts plus 13.

178

Sl 6 sts onto cable needle and hold at back, k2, p1, k2, then work sts from cable needle [p1, k2] twice.

※

Drop k st from needle to make a ladder, then work yo. (Run will stop at previous yo.)

Note that only rows 1-24 are repeated, foundation row is not. On last row make appropriate runs before binding off.

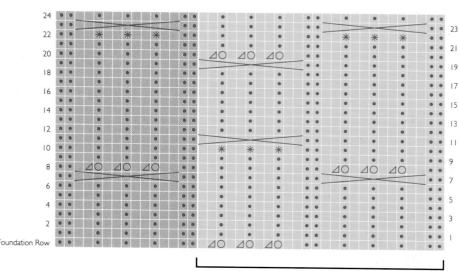

Multiple of 26 sts plus 15.

179

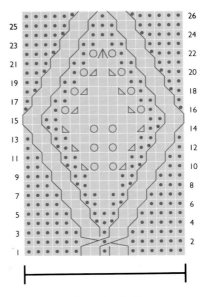

Panel of 17 sts.

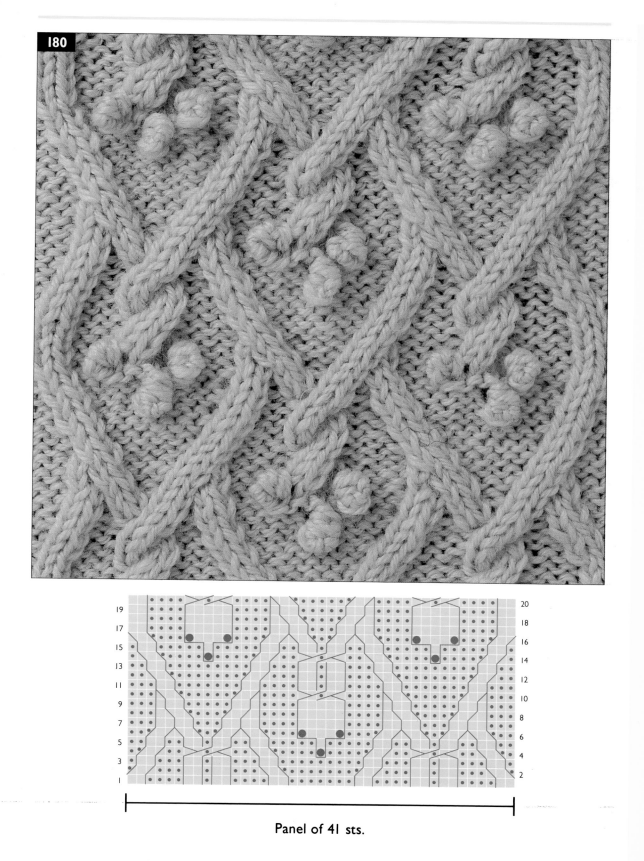

Panel of 41 sts.

181

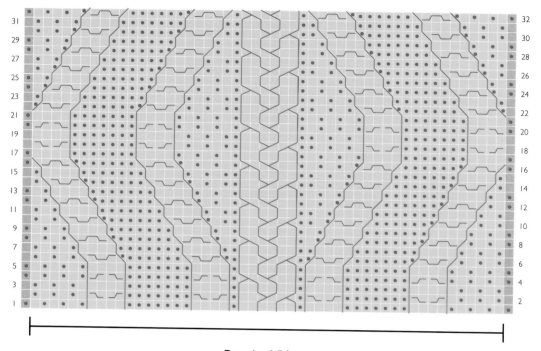

Panel of 50 sts.

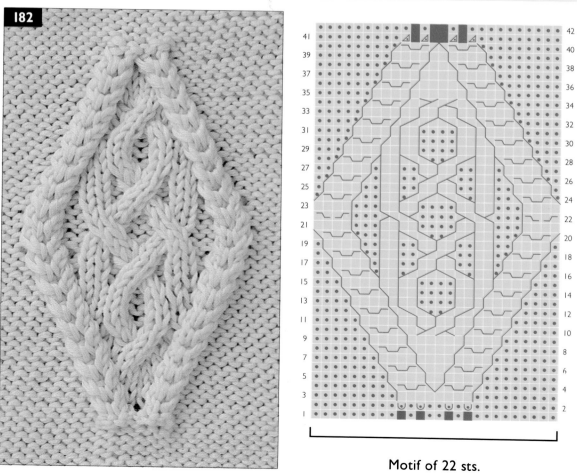

Motif of 22 sts.

183

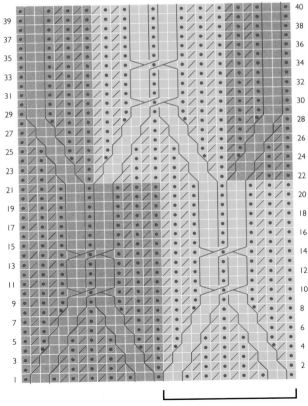

Multiple of 14 sts plus 15.

184

Panel of 90 sts.

LACE AND BOBBLE STITCHES

Both lace and bobble stitches are very compatible with cables and feature in the previous section. Here, I have used them together and separately, so that round, three-dimensional bobbles complement round, open eyelets.

There are many ways of making bobbles, but the basic principle I have used is that one stitch is increased into several times, the newly-formed group of stitches is then worked, and then the increased stitches are passed over the first one, which is worked again to "anchor" it. This gives a firm, round bobble without a tendency to disappear to the wrong side of the knitting. Single eyelets are made by decreasing one stitch and compensating for this with a yarn-over increase. Double eyelets are made by working two decreases with a double yarn over between. They can both be used to form an allover lacy fabric or to define a pattern on a solid ground.

Lace stitches are usually better worked on a largish needle and in a yarn which can be blocked (that is, shaped and pinned out) and thoroughly pressed.

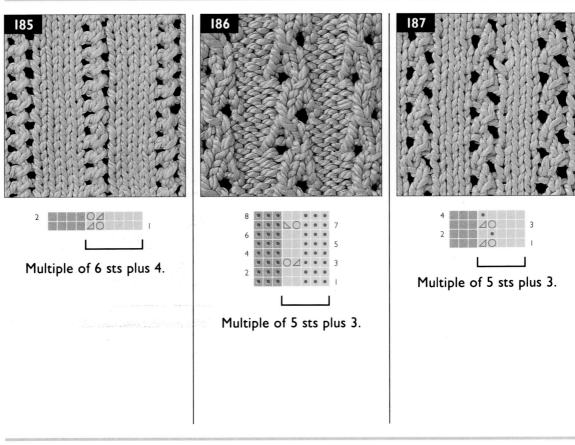

185

Multiple of 6 sts plus 4.

186

Multiple of 5 sts plus 3.

187

Multiple of 5 sts plus 3.

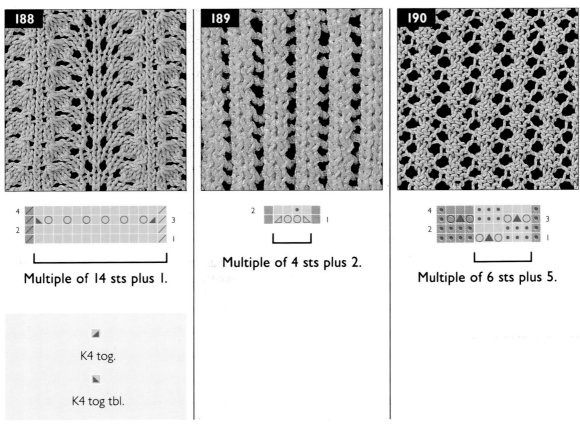

188

Multiple of 14 sts plus 1.

K4 tog.

K4 tog tbl.

189

Multiple of 4 sts plus 2.

190

Multiple of 6 sts plus 5.

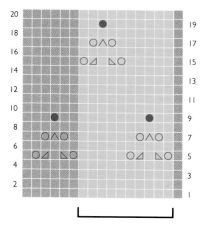

Multiple of 10 sts plus 7.

● (k1, yo, k1, yo, k1) in st to make 5 sts from 1, turn, p5, turn, k3, k2 tog, pass 3 sts, one at a time, over k2 tog.

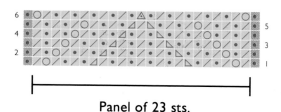

Panel of 23 sts.

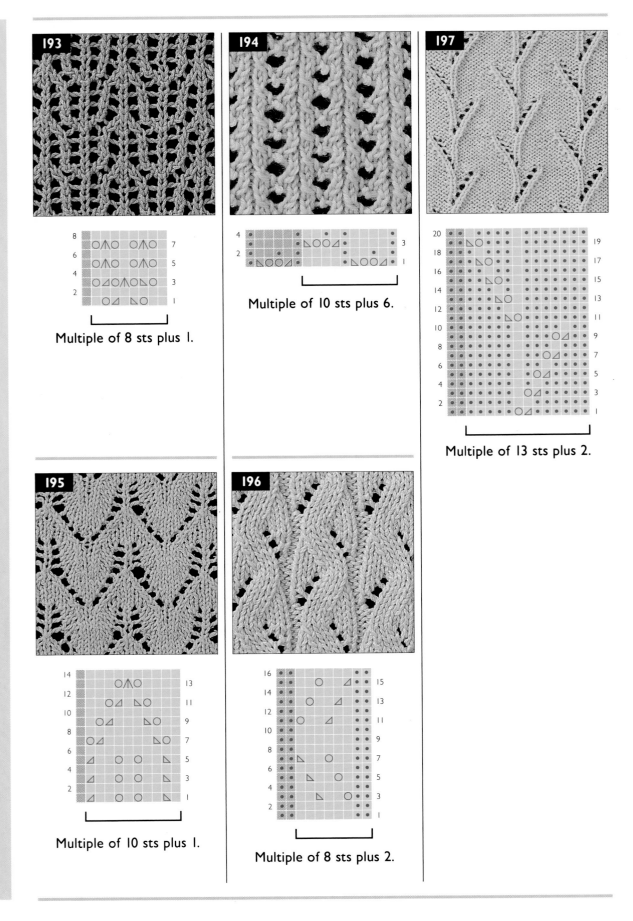

193

Multiple of 8 sts plus 1.

194

Multiple of 10 sts plus 6.

197

Multiple of 13 sts plus 2.

195

Multiple of 10 sts plus 1.

196

Multiple of 8 sts plus 2.

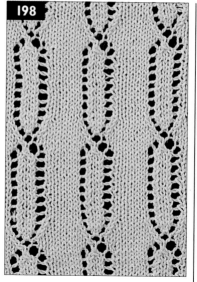

198

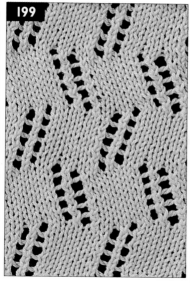

199

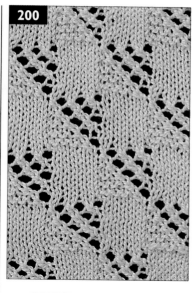

200

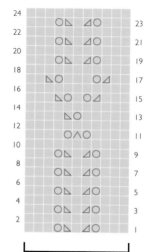

Multiple of 11 sts.

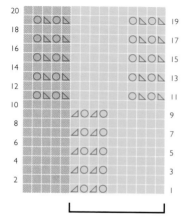

Multiple of 10 sts plus 5.

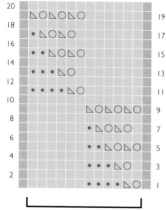

Multiple of 12 sts plus 2.

201

202

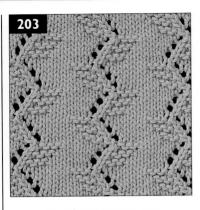

203

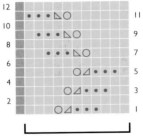

Multiple of 11 sts plus 1.

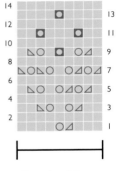

Panel of 9 sts.

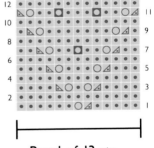

Panel of 13 sts.

▣ (K1, p1, k1, p1, k1) in st to make 5 sts from 1, turn, k5, turn, pass 2nd, 3rd, 4th, and 5th sts over first st, k in back of this st.

204

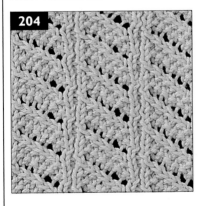

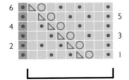

Multiple of 9 sts plus 1.

205

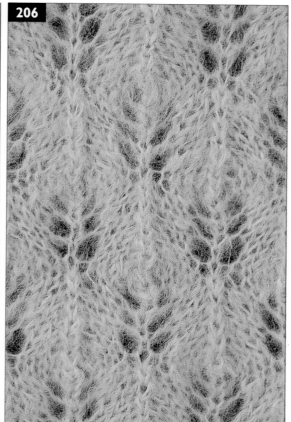

206

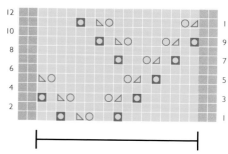

Panel of 17 sts.

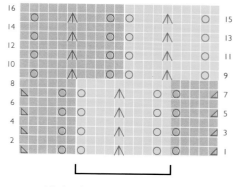

Multiple of 10 sts plus 11.

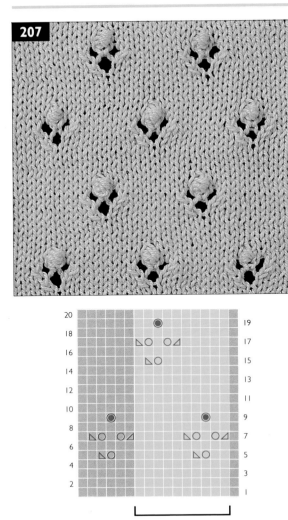

207

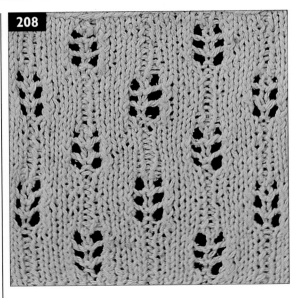

208

Multiple of 10 sts plus 7.

Multiple of 12 sts plus 7.

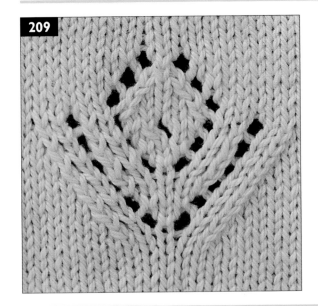

209

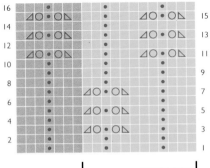

Motif of 17 sts.

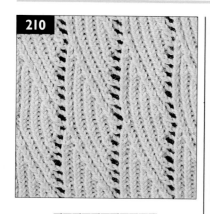

210

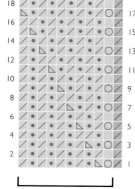

Multiple of 10 sts plus 1.

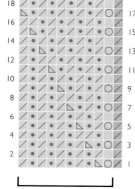

K2 tog *through back of loops.*

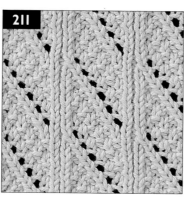

211

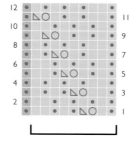

Multiple of 9 sts plus 1.

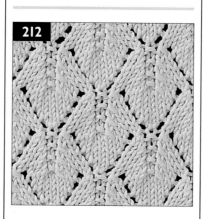

212

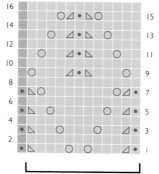

Multiple of 12 sts plus 1.

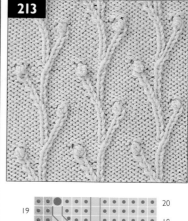

213

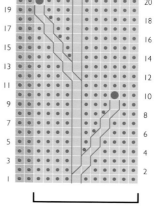

Multiple of 11 sts plus 2.

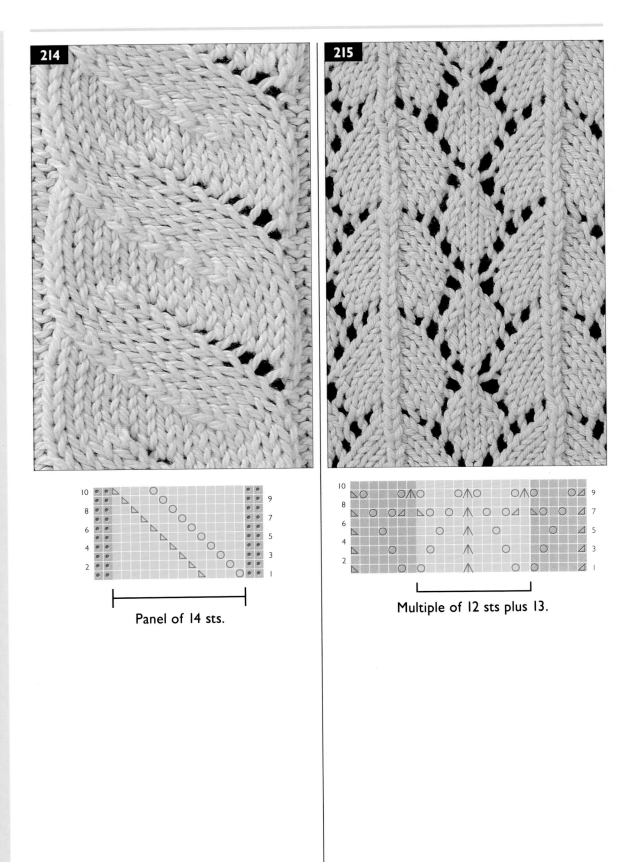

214

215

Panel of 14 sts.

Multiple of 12 sts plus 13.

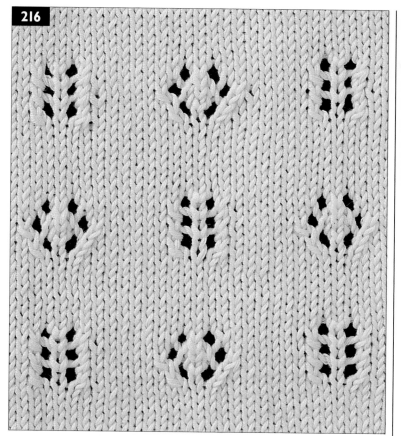

216

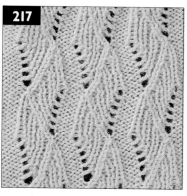

217

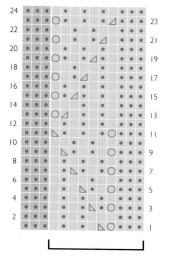

Multiple of 10 sts plus 3.

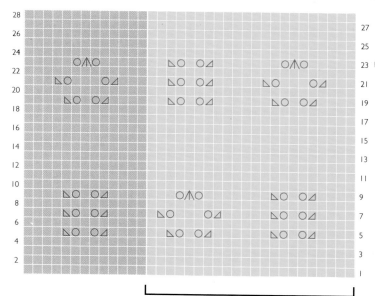

Multiple of 22 sts plus 13.

218

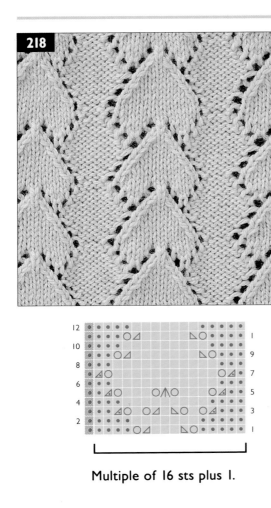

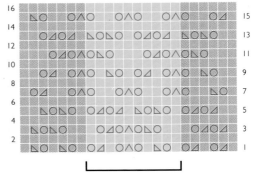

Multiple of 16 sts plus 1.

219

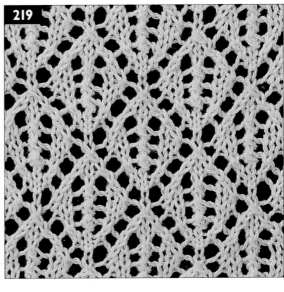

Multiple of 10 sts plus 13.

220

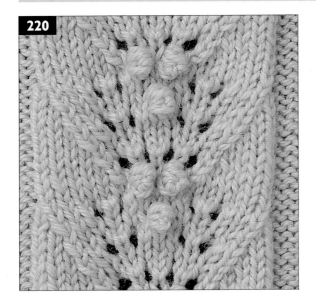

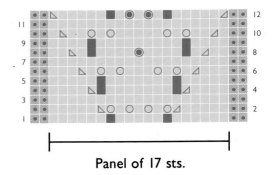

Panel of 17 sts.

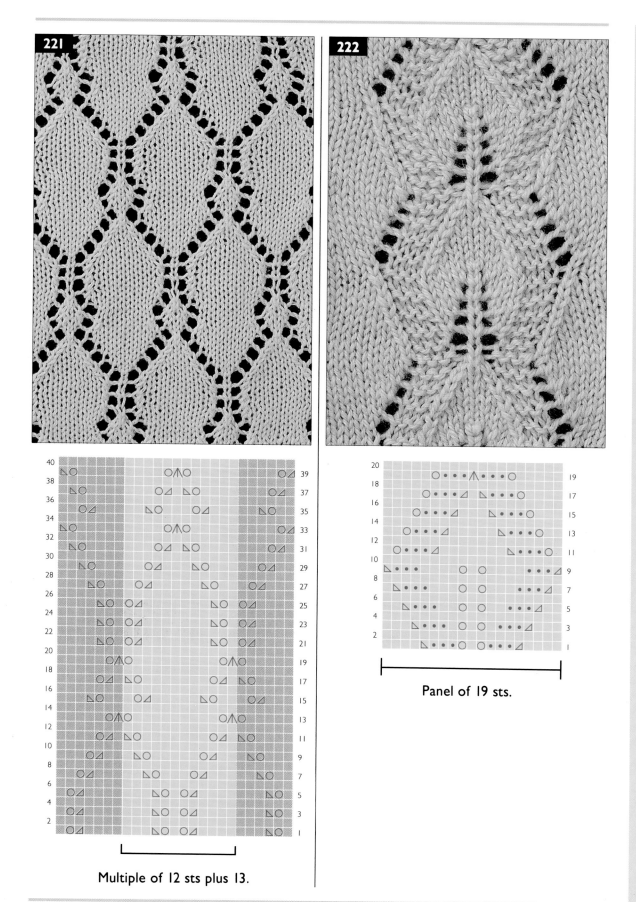

221

222

Multiple of 12 sts plus 13.

Panel of 19 sts.

135

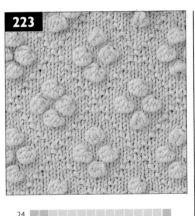

223

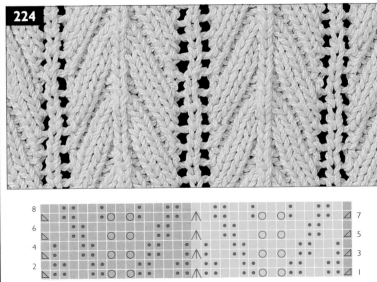

224

Multiple of 16 sts plus 17.

Multiple of 12 sts plus 3.

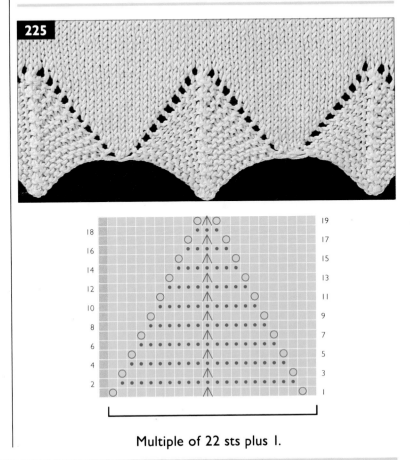

225

Multiple of 22 sts plus 1.

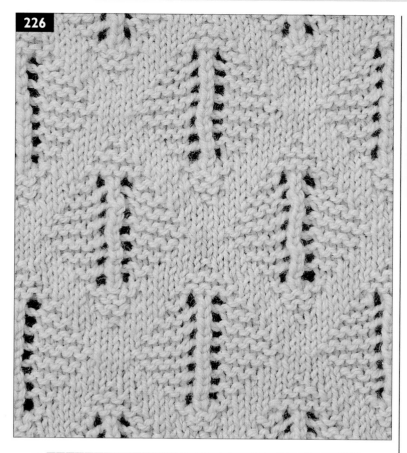

226

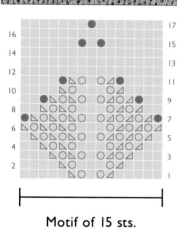

227

Motif of 15 sts.

Multiple of 16 sts plus 17.

228

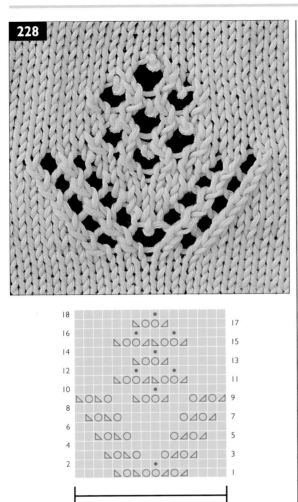

Motif of 16 sts.

229

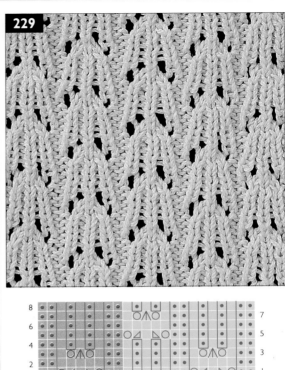

Multiple of 14 sts plus 9.

230

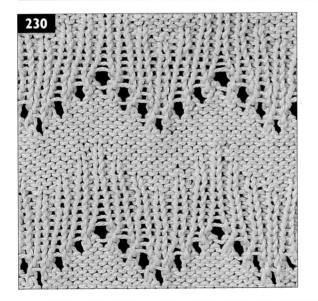

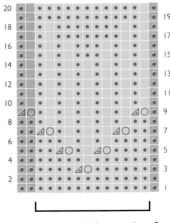

Multiple of 12 sts plus 3.

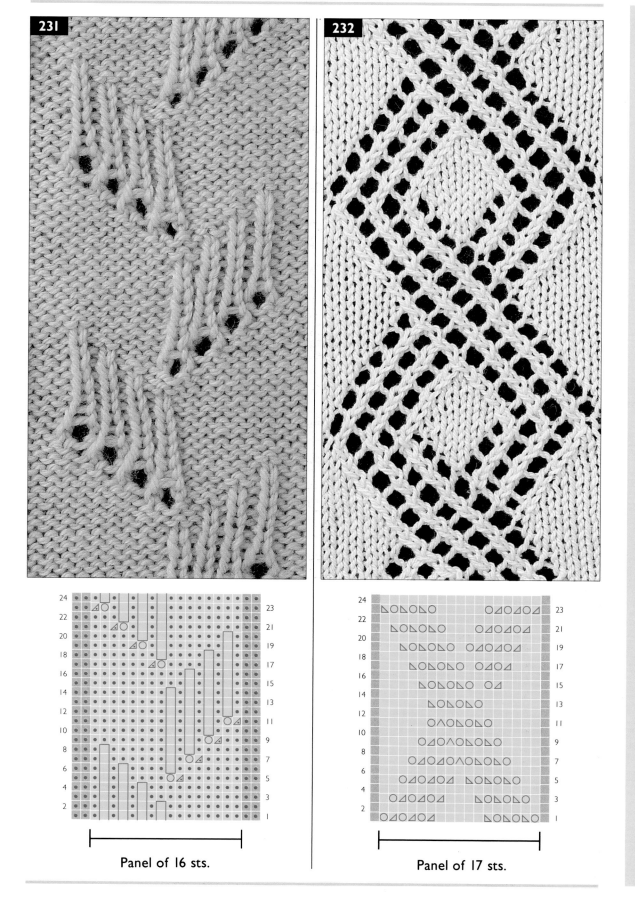

231

232

Panel of 16 sts.

Panel of 17 sts.

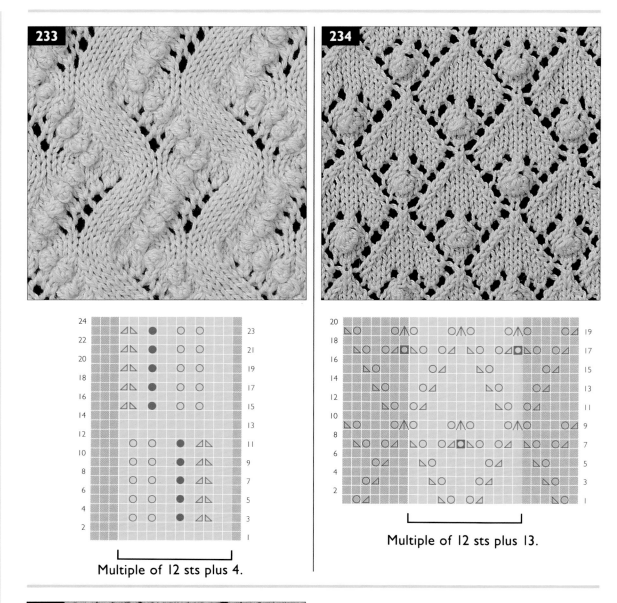

233

Multiple of 12 sts plus 4.

234

Multiple of 12 sts plus 13.

235

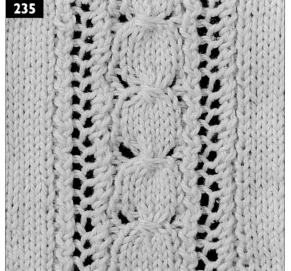

Panel of 18 sts.

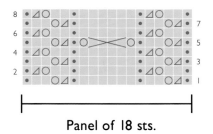

Sl next 3 sts onto right-hand needle, k in front and back of next st, k2, pass 3 slipped sts over 4 sts just worked.

236

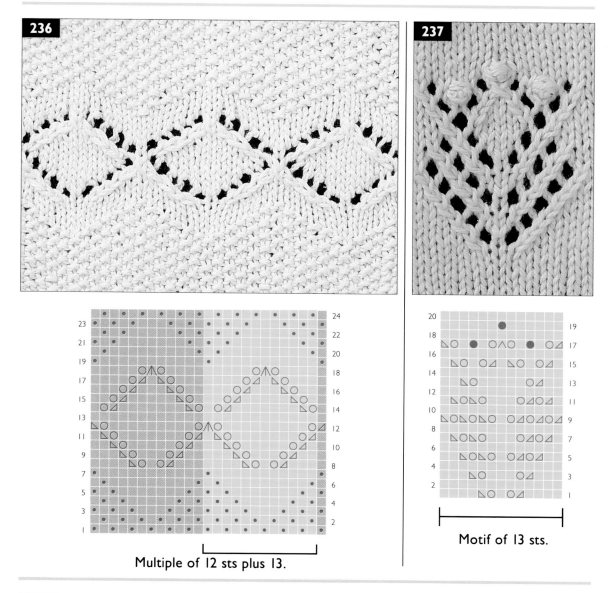

Multiple of 12 sts plus 13.

237

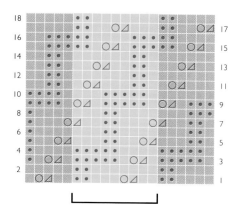

Motif of 13 sts.

238

Multiple of 9 sts plus 11.

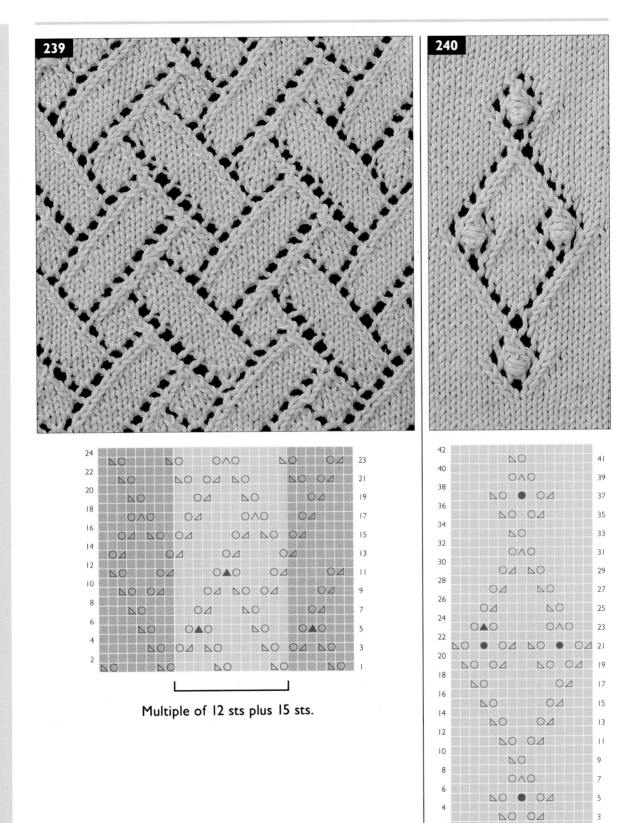

239

240

Multiple of 12 sts plus 15 sts.

Motif of 15 sts.

241

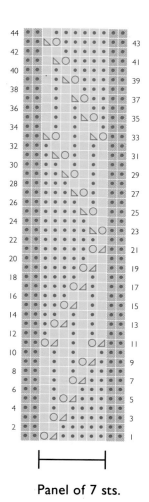

Panel of 7 sts.

242

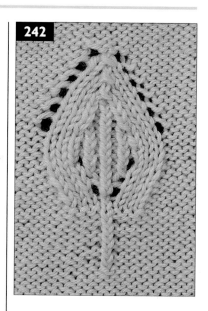

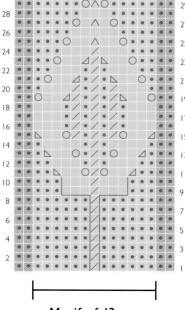

Motif of 13 sts.

243

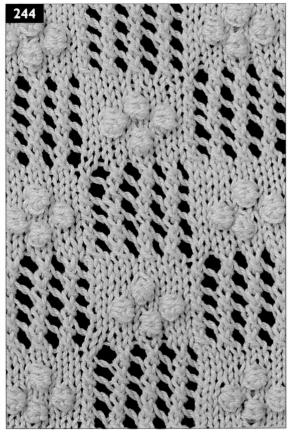

244

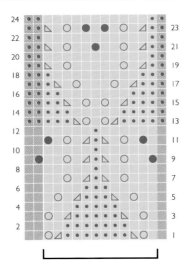

Multiple of 12 sts plus 3.

Multiple of 16 sts plus 9.

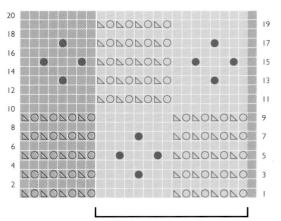

(K1, p1, k1, p1, k1, p1, k1) in st to make 7 sts from 1, pass 2nd, 3rd, 4th, 5th, 6th, and 7th sts, one at a time, over first st.

245

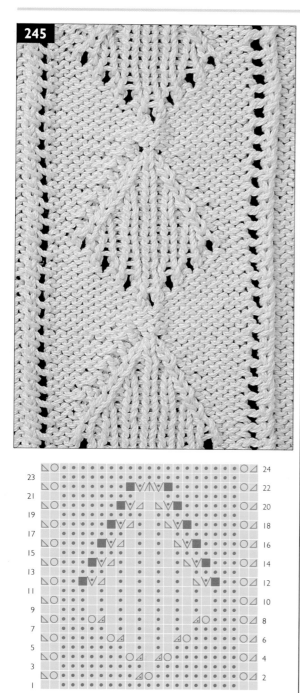

246

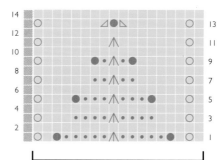

Multiple of 18 sts plus 1.

Panel of 23 sts.

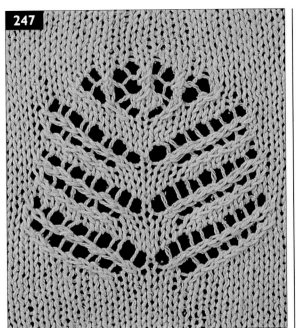

247

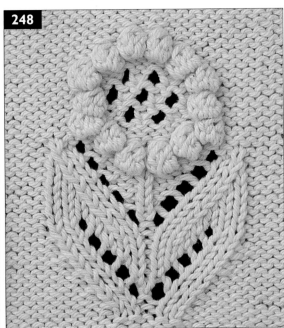

248

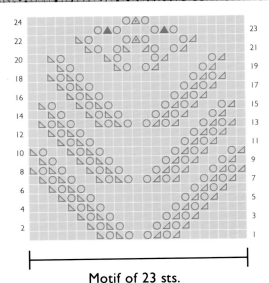

Motif of 23 sts.

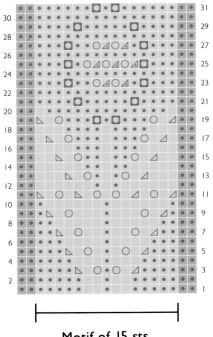

Motif of 15 sts.

249

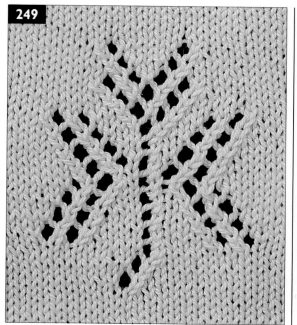

250

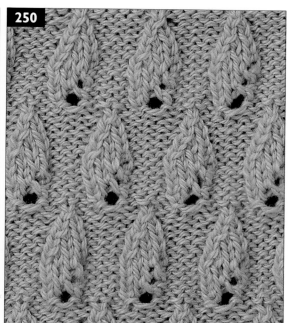

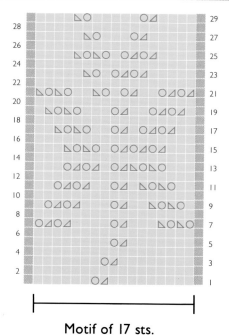

Motif of 17 sts.

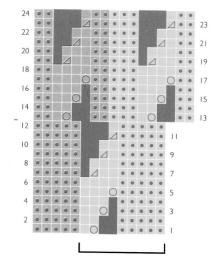

Multiple of 6 sts plus 5.

251

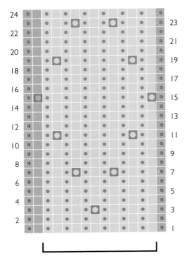

Multiple of 12 sts plus 3.

252

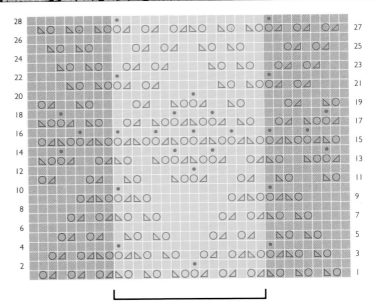

Multiple of 16 sts plus 18.

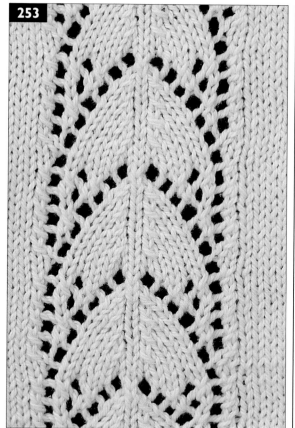

253

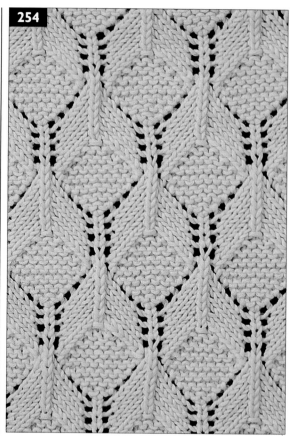

254

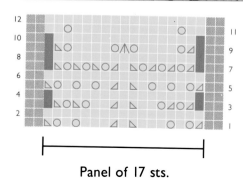

Panel of 17 sts.

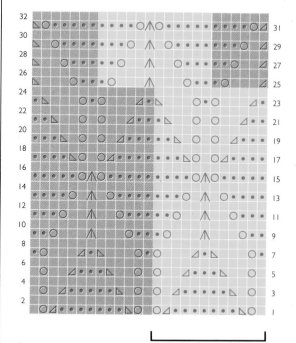

Multiple of 12 sts plus 13.

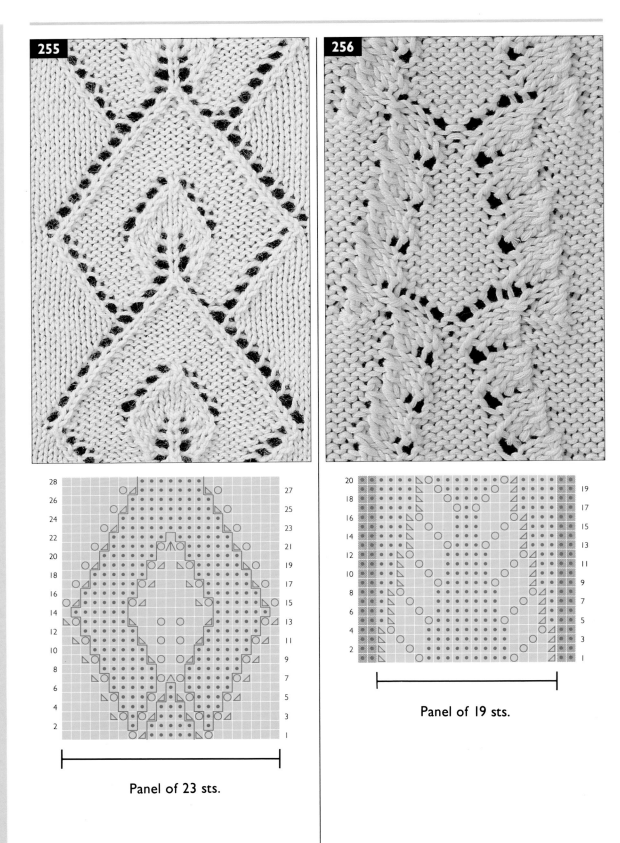

255

256

Panel of 23 sts.

Panel of 19 sts.

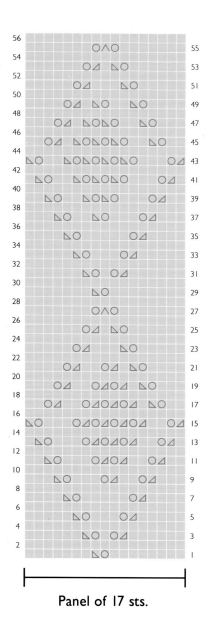

Panel of 17 sts.

257

258

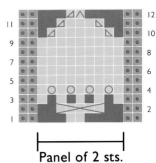

Panel of 2 sts.

SI 1 st onto cable needle
and hold at front, [k1, yo]
twice, then k1 st from cable
needle.

259

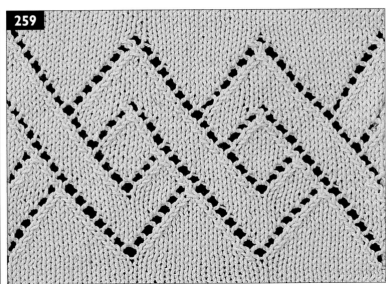

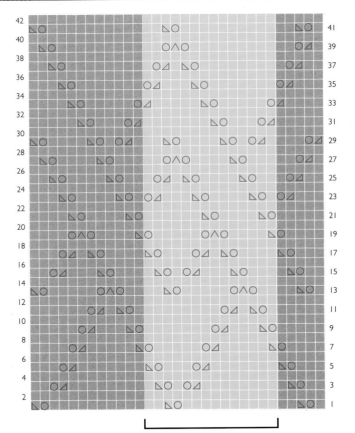

Multiple of 14 sts plus 17.

260

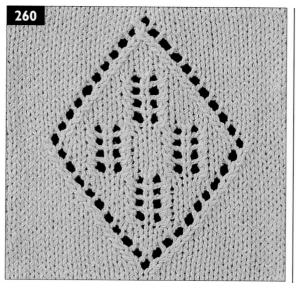

261

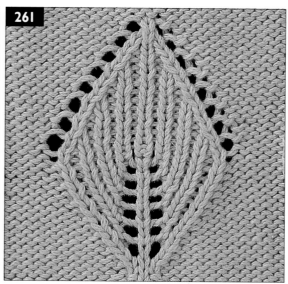

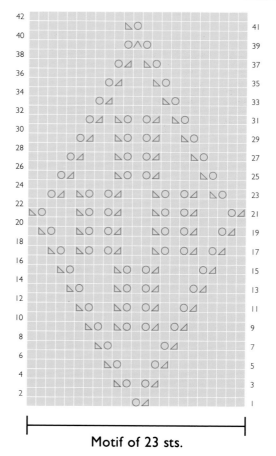

Motif of 23 sts.

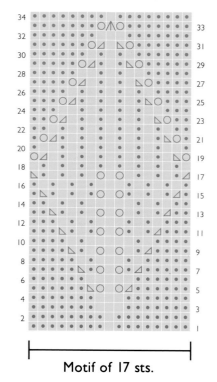

Motif of 17 sts.

LACE AND BOBBLE STITCHES

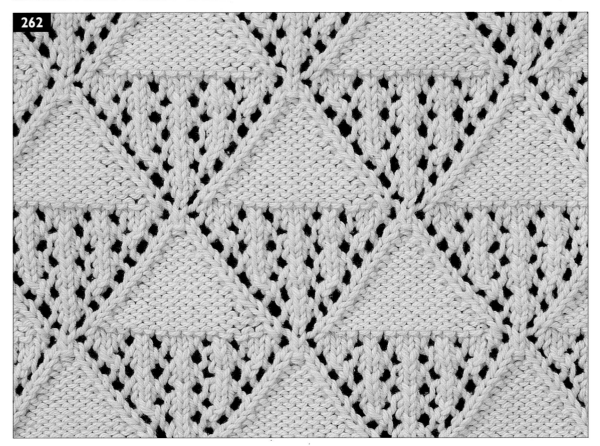

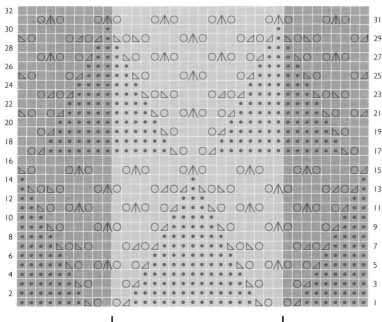

Multiple of 18 sts plus 19.

263

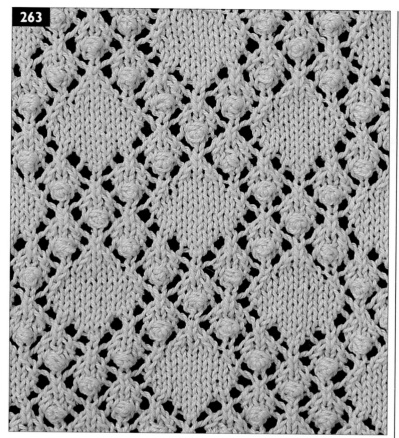

264

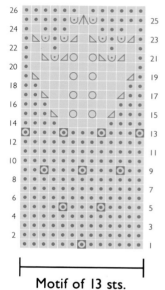

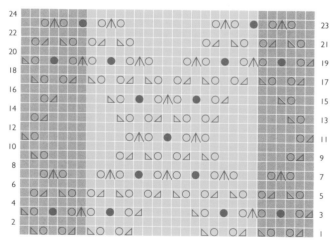

Multiple of 18 sts plus 13.

Motif of 13 sts.

265

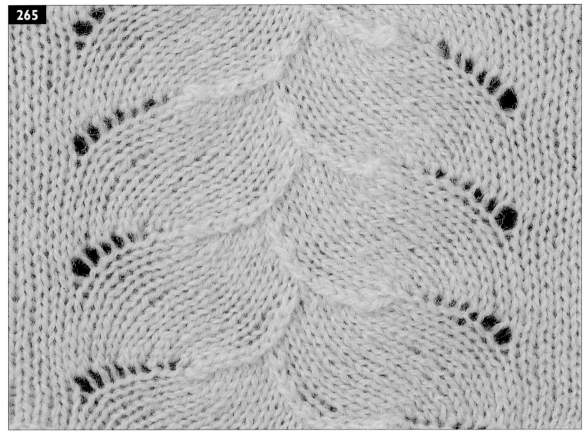

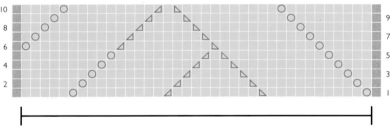

Panel of 37 sts.

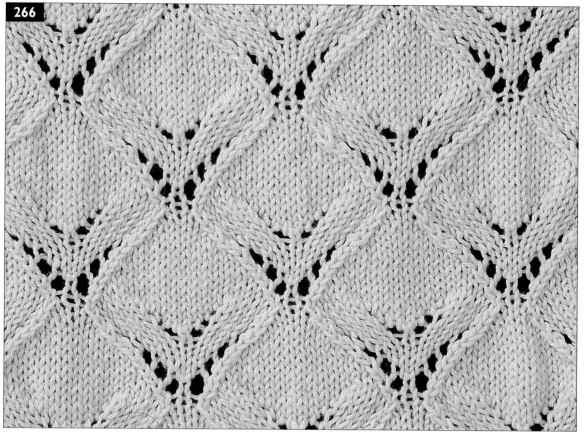

266

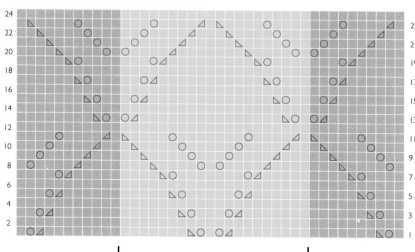

Multiple of 20 sts plus 21.

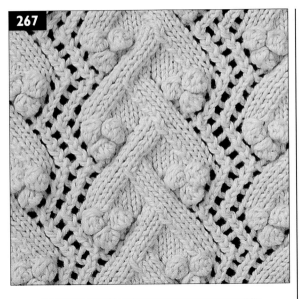

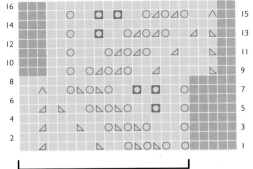

Multiple of 18 sts plus 5.

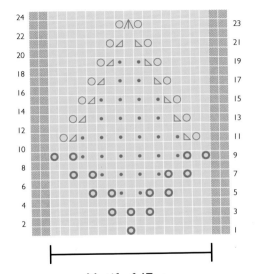

Motif of 17 sts.

158

269

270

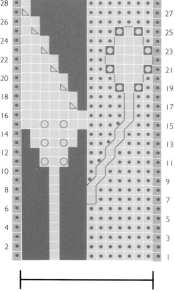

Motif of 8 sts.

Panel of 26 sts.

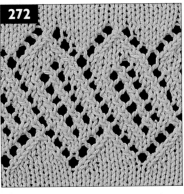

271

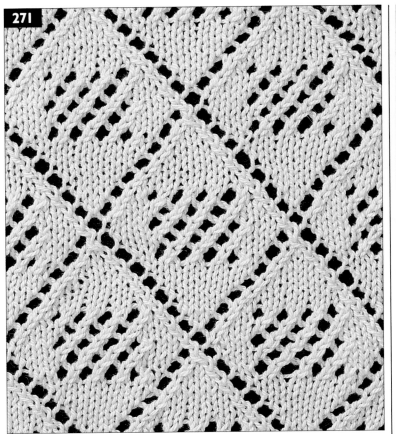

272

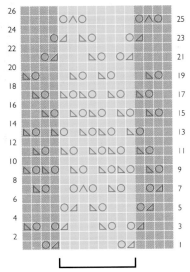

Multiple of 8 sts plus 8.

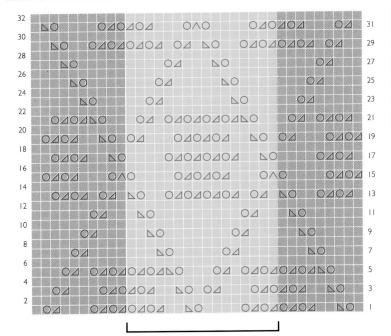

Multiple of 16 sts plus 19.

273

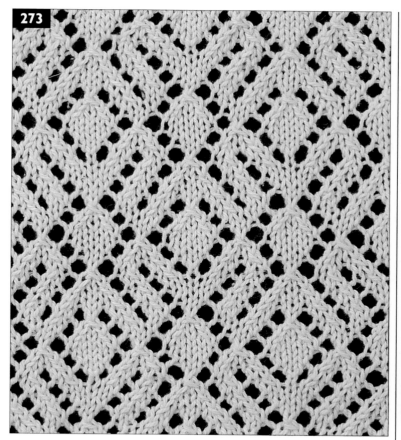

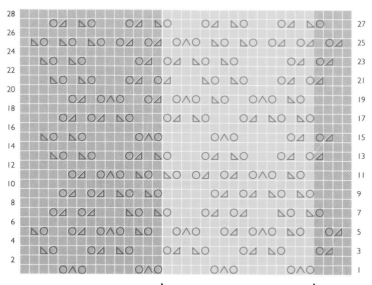

Multiple of 16 sts plus 19.

274

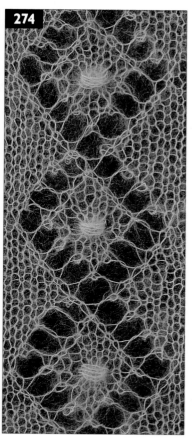

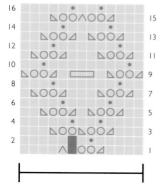

Panel of 13 sts.

275

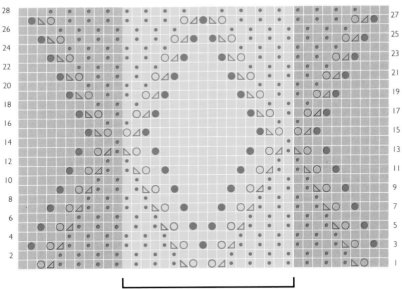

Multiple of 18 sts plus 21.

276

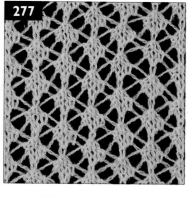

277

Multiple of 6 sts plus 6.

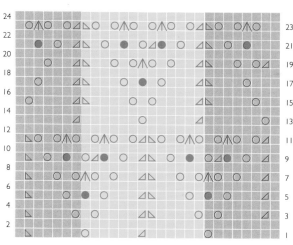

Multiple of 13 sts plus 15.

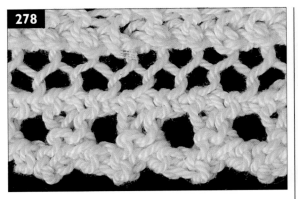

278

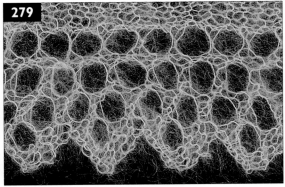

279

Cast on 6 sts.

Cast on 11 sts.

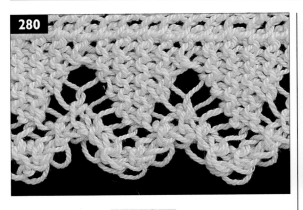

280

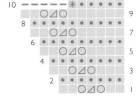

281

Cast on 7 sts.

Cast on 6 sts.

282

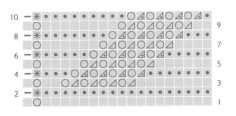

Cast on 19 sts.

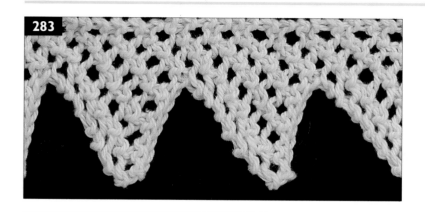

283

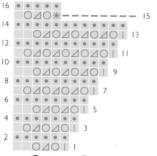

Cast on 5 sts.

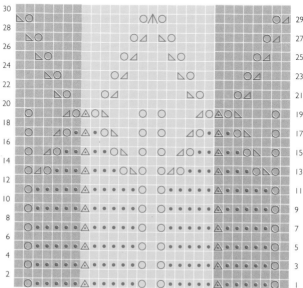

284

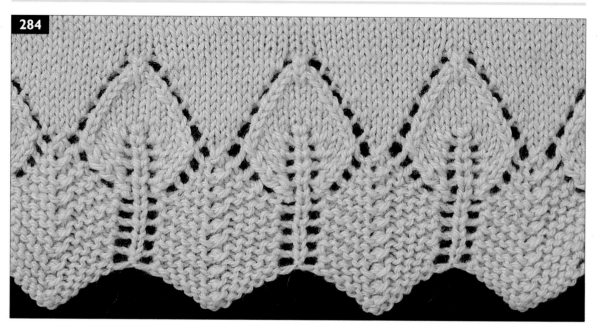

Multiple of 14 sts plus 15.

285

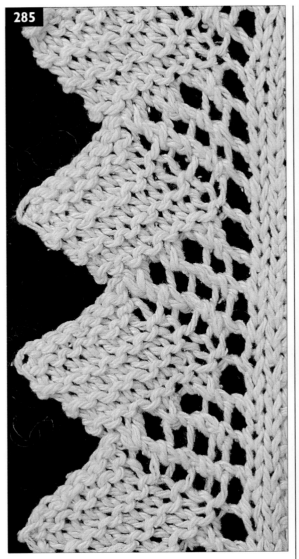

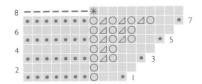

Cast on 10 sts.

286

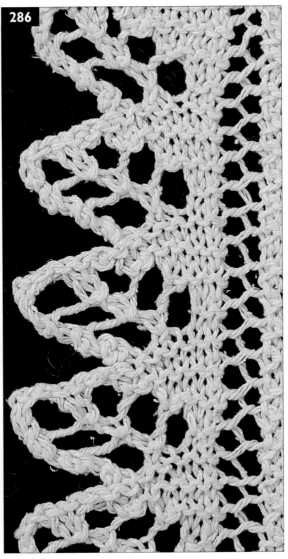

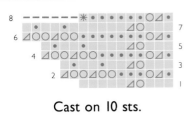

Cast on 10 sts.

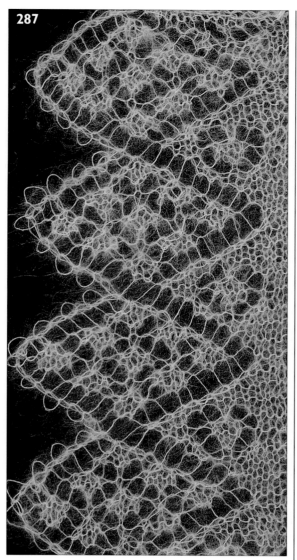

287

288

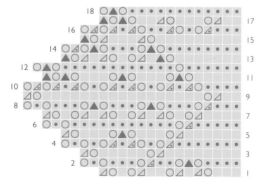

Cast on 15 sts.

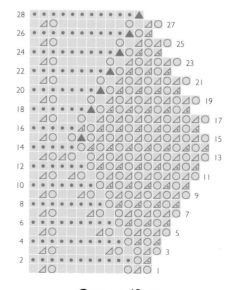

Cast on 12 sts.

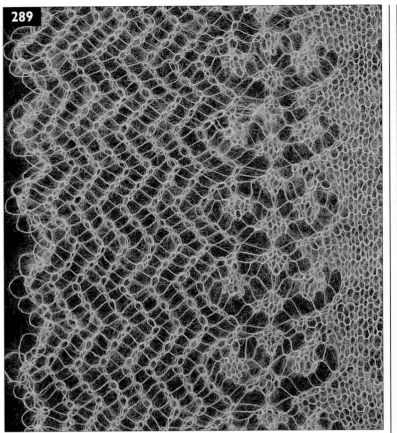

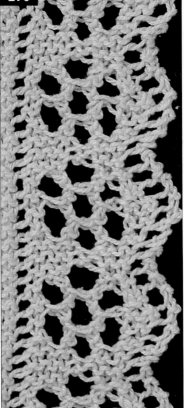

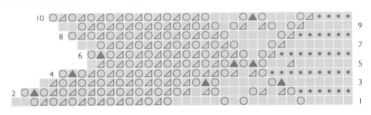

Cast on 32 sts.

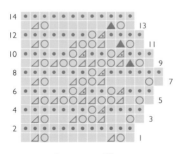

Cast on 12 sts.

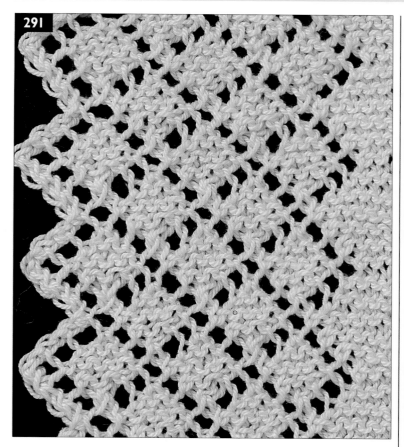

291

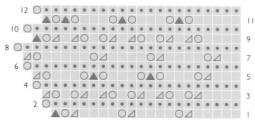

Cast on 22 sts.

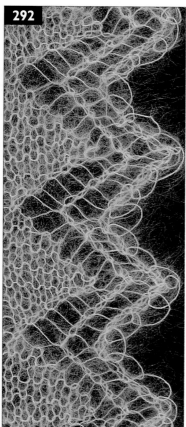

292

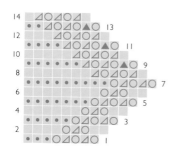

Cast on 7 sts.

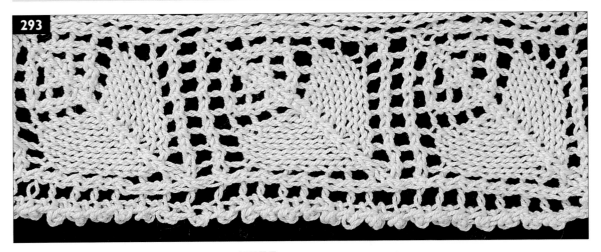

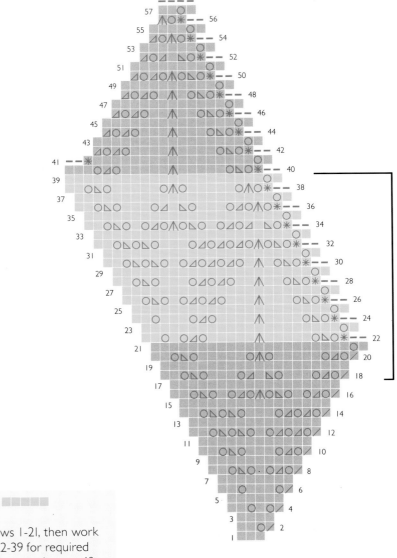

Cast on 3 sts.

Work rows 1-21, then work
rows 22-39 for required
length, then work rows 40-
57, cast off remaining
4 sts.

294

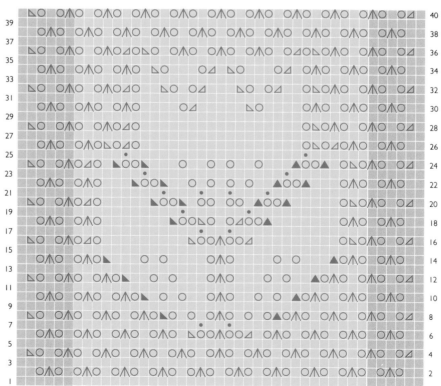

Motif of 31 sts.

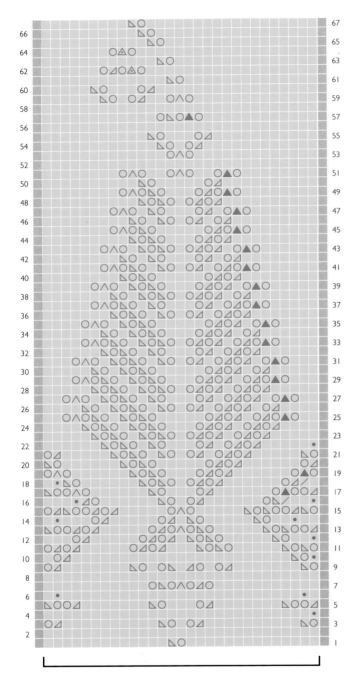

Multiple of 29 sts plus 2.

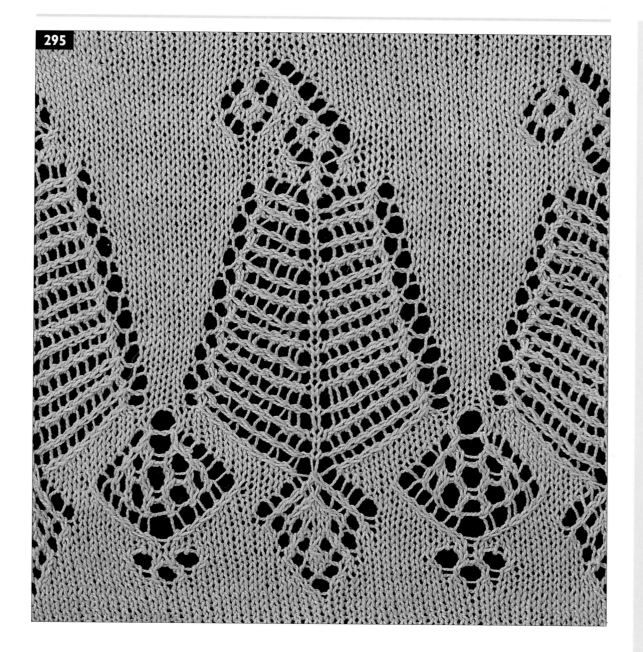

TWISTED AND OTHER STITCHES

Twisting two stitches by working the second before the first gives a similar appearance to a one-over-one cable but has the advantage that a cable needle isn't required and so large areas of twisted stitches can be worked where it would be tedious to cable. Although not quite so well-defined as cables, twisted stitches (also called "crossed stitches") give a linear, raised texture to the surface of the knitting and also contract the fabric. This can be compensated for by working increases below and decreases above the twisted stitch areas, or stitches such as eyelets can be used to open up the fabric.

Another method of embossing is to work multiple increases which raise the surface of the knitting. The shapes that result can be designed to look like leaves and fruit and so extend the possibilities of making pictures without using color.

296

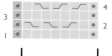

Multiple of 6 sts plus 3.
This stitch is reversible.

297

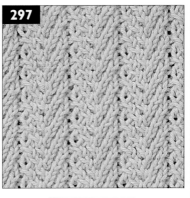

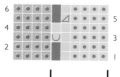

Multiple of 8 sts plus 1.

298

Multiple of 5 sts plus 4.

299

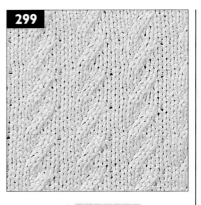

Multiple of 7 sts.

300

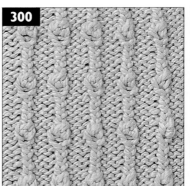

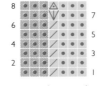

Multiple of 4 sts plus 3.

301

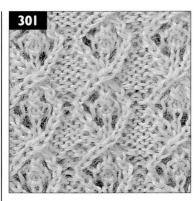

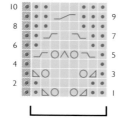

Multiple of 8 sts plus 1.

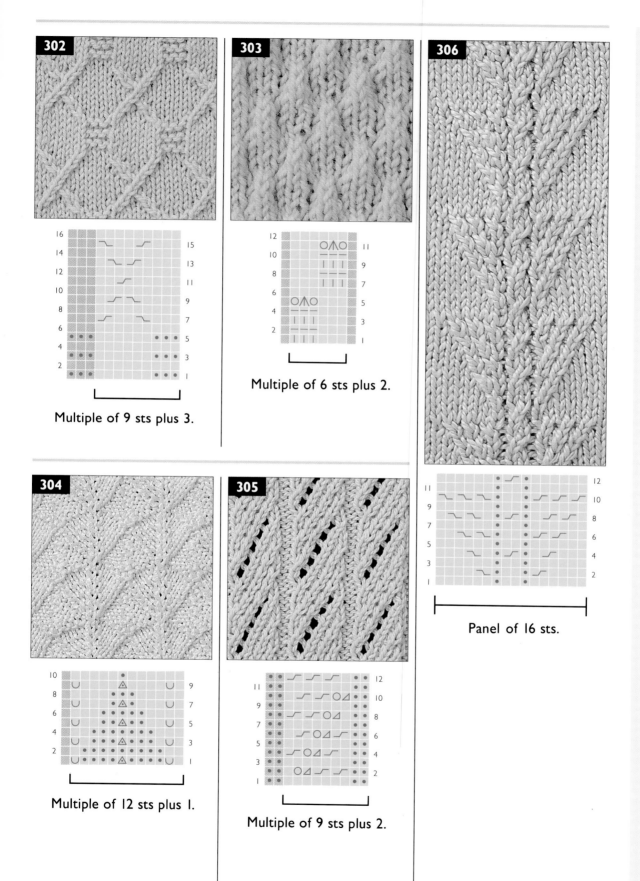

302

16
15
14
13
12
11
10
9
8
7
6
5
4
3
2
1

Multiple of 9 sts plus 3.

303

12
11
10
9
8
7
6
5
4
3
2
1

Multiple of 6 sts plus 2.

306

11
12
9
10
7
8
5
6
3
4
1
2

Panel of 16 sts.

304

10
9
8
7
6
5
4
3
2
1

Multiple of 12 sts plus 1.

305

11
12
9
10
7
8
5
6
3
4
1
2

Multiple of 9 sts plus 2.

TWISTED AND OTHER STITCHES

307

Multiple of 10 sts.

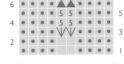

(K1, p1, k1, p1, k1) in st to
make 5 sts from 1.

5

K5 on RS rows, p5 on WS
rows.

▲

P5 tog.

308

Multiple of 12 sts plus 6.

309

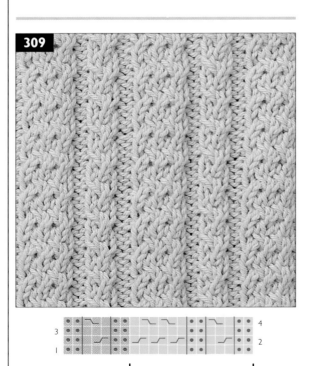

Multiple of 13 sts plus 7.

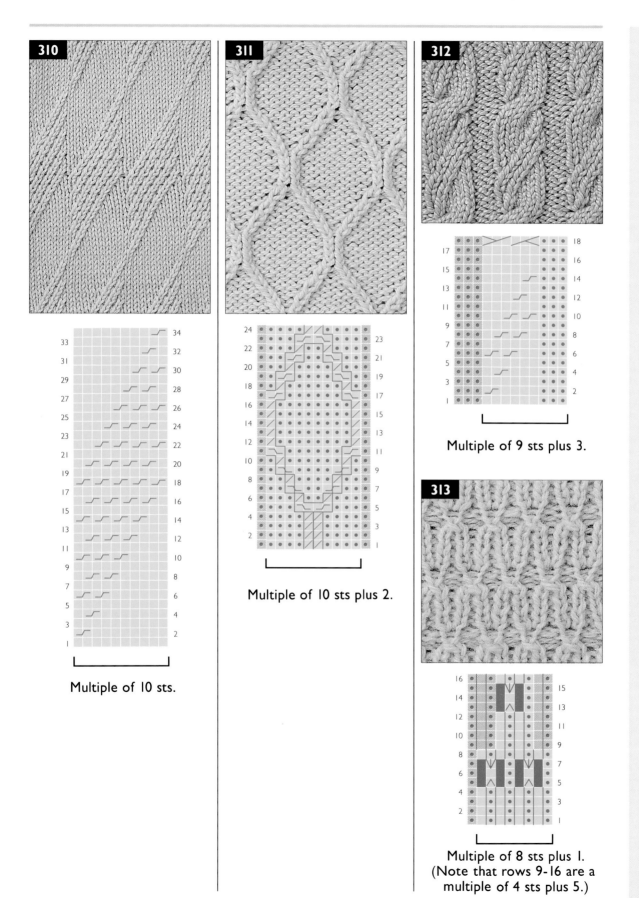

310

Multiple of 10 sts.

311

Multiple of 10 sts plus 2.

312

Multiple of 9 sts plus 3.

313

Multiple of 8 sts plus 1.
(Note that rows 9-16 are a
multiple of 4 sts plus 5.)

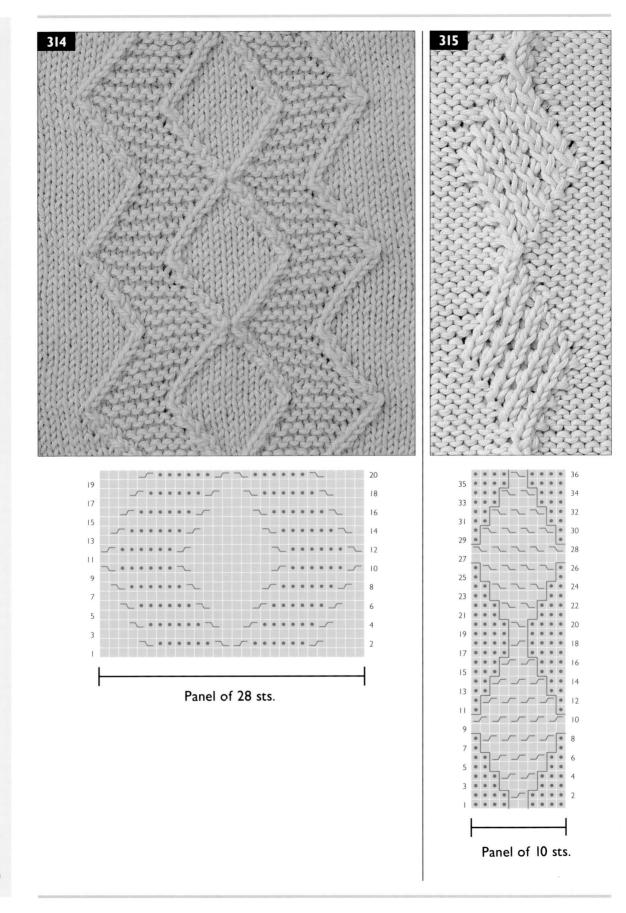

314

Panel of 28 sts.

315

Panel of 10 sts.

316

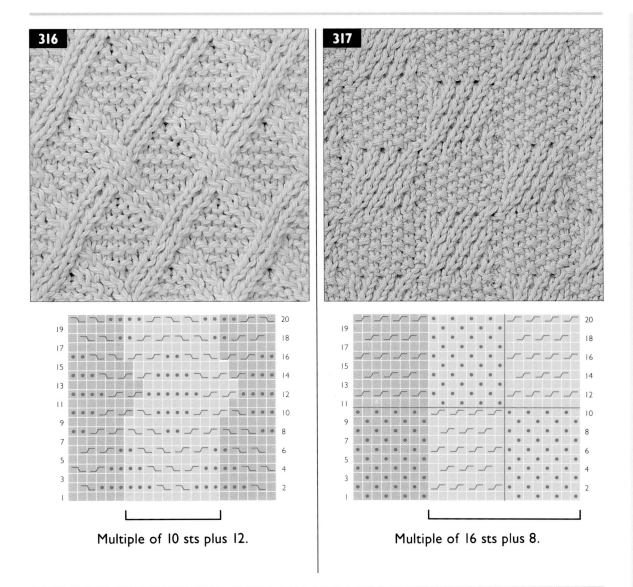

Multiple of 10 sts plus 12.

317

Multiple of 16 sts plus 8.

318

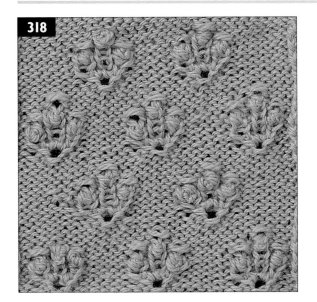

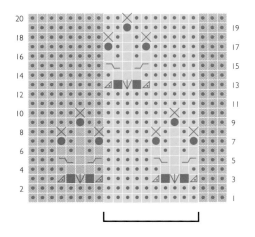

Multiple of 10 sts plus 11.

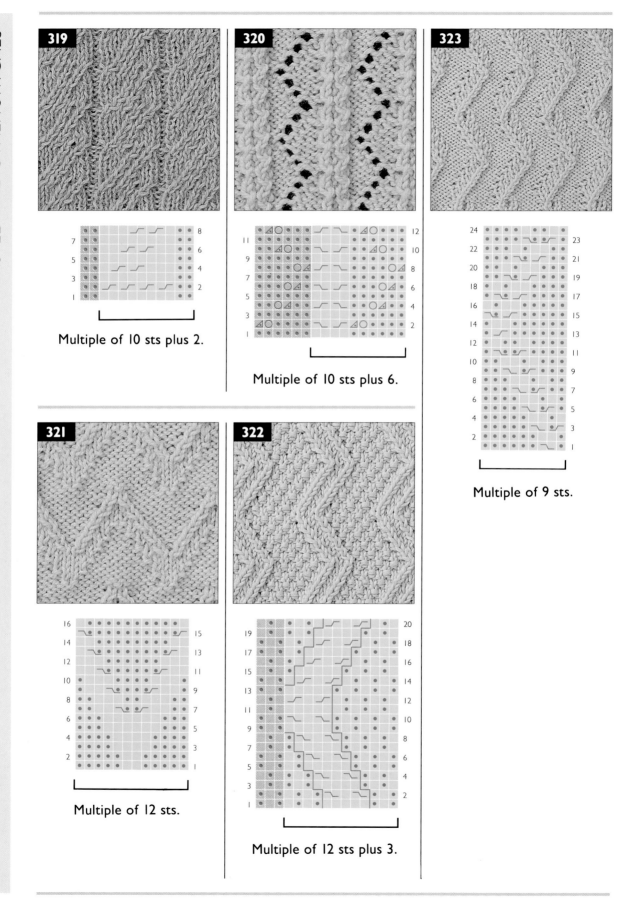

Multiple of 10 sts plus 2.

Multiple of 10 sts plus 6.

Multiple of 9 sts.

Multiple of 12 sts.

Multiple of 12 sts plus 3.

324

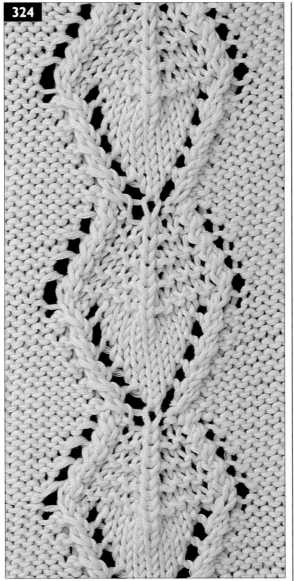

325

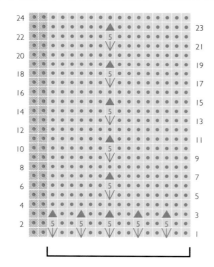

Multiple of 15 sts plus 2.

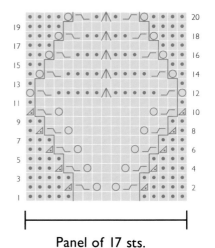

Panel of 17 sts.

$\mathbb{V}$

(P1, k1, p1, k1, p1) in st to make 5 sts from 1.

5

K5.

▲

With yarn at back, sl 4 sts purlwise, p1, take 4 slipped sts over p1.

326

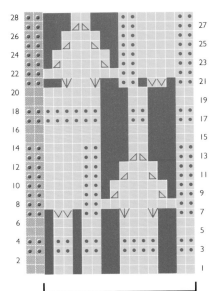

Multiple of 10 sts plus 2.

327

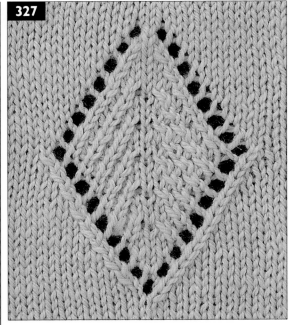

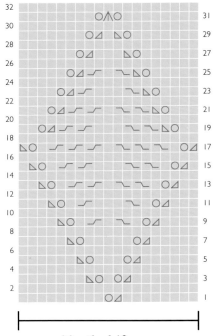

Motif of 19 sts.

328

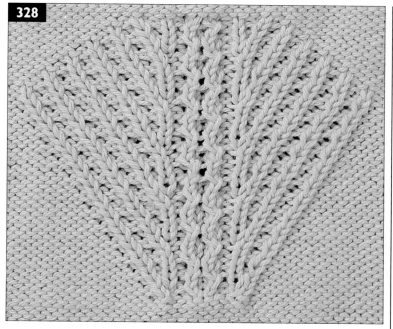

329

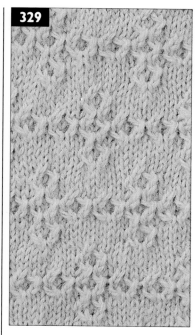

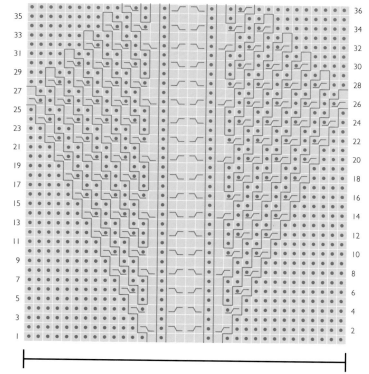

Motif of 34 sts.

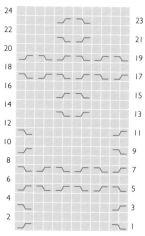

Multiple of 12 sts.

330

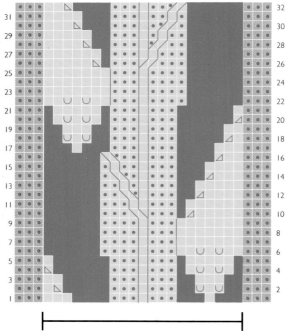

Panel of 11 sts.

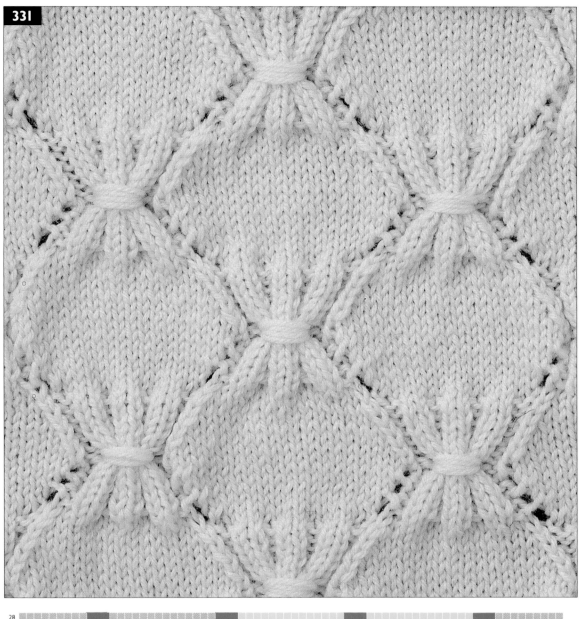

331

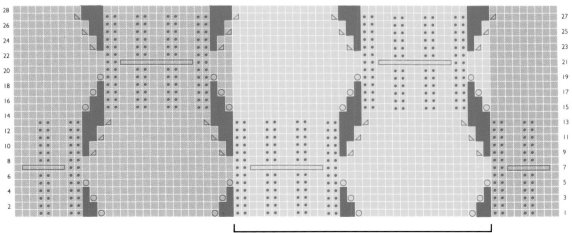

Multiple of 28 sts plus 32.

Chart A

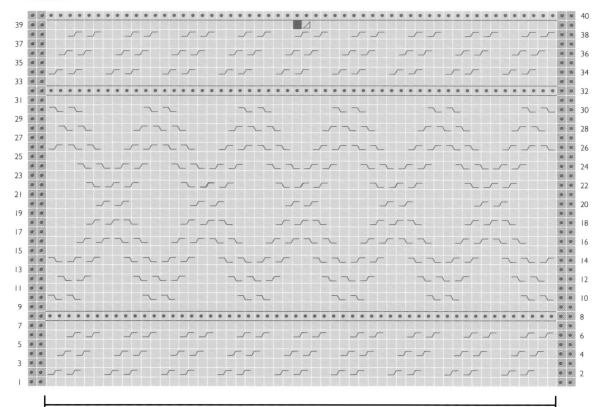

Chart A is worked first and is
a motif of 54 sts, decreased
to 53 sts on row 39.
Chart B is then worked
consecutively, the motif
starting with 53 sts on row
41. The stitch count then
varies until 53 sts are
resumed on row 106.

Chart B

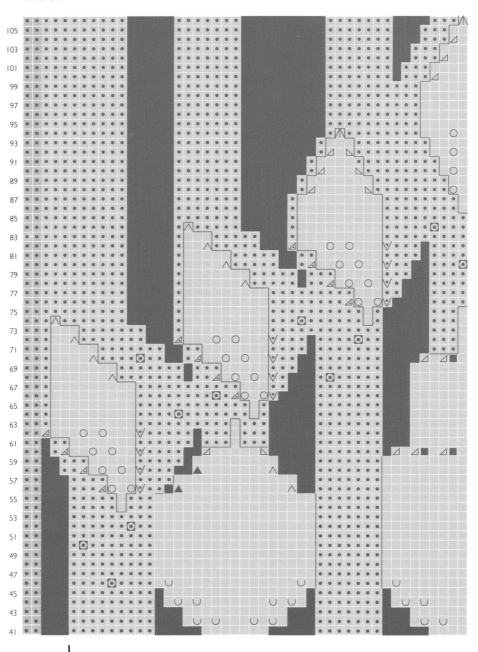

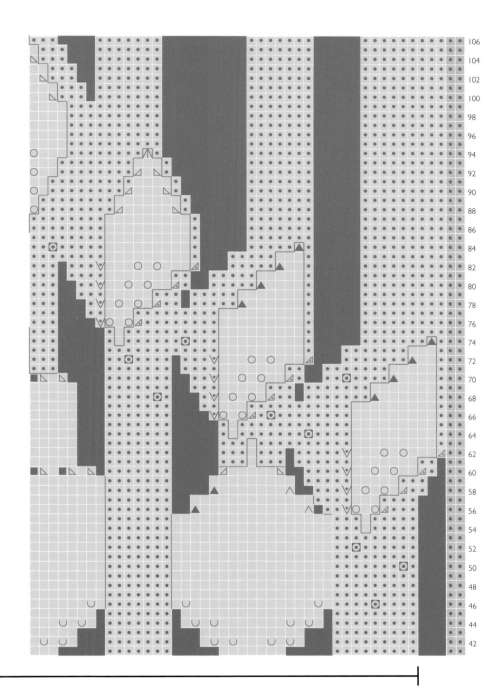